ARTIST SALES

KIT

Techniques, instructions, examples and

exercises to encourage and empower

all creative artists to sell their own work

Published 2023 by Urban Viking

www.urbanviking.tv

Cover design by Andrea Fox

SUMMARY & INTRODUCTION

Every artist can find useful information in this book. This includes fine artists as well as craftsmen. Be it writing, photography, painting, sculpture, filmmaking, music, illustration, welding, printmaking, woodworking, glass working, or other creative endeavor: every artist wants to sell their work.

In my years working as a filmmaker, I have met artists from a variety of disciplines. After hearing many horror stories about how difficult these artists' journeys have been, I began to recognize a common mistake: By putting so much time and effort into learning their craft and perfecting it, lots of artists do not have the experience or know-how to effectively sell their art. I can now see that so many artists lack the necessary business sense to market and sell their work professionally. It is with these people in mind that I began writing The Artist Sales Kit.

After meeting with an artist, I often find myself puzzling over what exactly it is that this person does and to whom they are marketing their work. This is because many artists have never had to explain what they do to a layperson. Part of this imprecision is due to a lack of sales and marketing skill, which is essentially looking at your product from an outsider's perspective and figuring out how best to represent your product to this perspective. That said, I believe I have found the root of the "starving artist" truism: Artists have no clue how to generate income from their work to manage their daily living expenses. I am aware that creative people have very little interest in the "How-To" process of sales. Yet, I also know that all artists need to eat and have a roof over their heads.

Introversion is common in creative spirits and sometimes this makes it difficult to speak directly about creative projects to the general public. However, communication is paramount to good sales. Artists should know how to pitch their ideas, network with industry people, and make a lasting impression. The artist must also be able to communicate to others what they do and who they are. It is very important to communicate with clarity, confidence, and preparation. Master effective communication and you will attract customers that are not only interested in your work, but willing to make a purchase. In this book, you will find sections dedicated solely to good business language, including lists of buzz words for resumes and advertisements. In addition, we break down sales letter writing and the entire processes of marketing and sales.

The Artist's Sales Kit will offer the artist real, useable marketing and sales principles and techniques to educate on the business side of art. Having the ability to network, market and sell your work and yourself is crucial to your survival and the longevity of your career. By integrating some of these basic skills, I can help the artist be proactive in selling and marketing their art and not have to rely on outsourcing to high-priced marketing agencies. This book is not trying to transform the artist into a salesperson; its function is solely to give you some simple tips and techniques to save you money and time.

Not all artists want to learn to market and sell their work. However, as an artist myself, I found that learning basic business skills gave me more confidence in life, the ability to systematically pitch my work in any situation, and control over the exposition of my work. These tips and techniques will prepare you to be more organized and to design a sales and marketing plan specific to your work. Practicing the outlined techniques will make it easier for you to sell your own work and learn more about the sales and distribution process at the same time.

It's time for you to take your artistic career seriously. By purchasing and reading The Artist's Sales Kit, you are already one step ahead of your competition. Let's get started!

Table of Contents

WORDS

POWER WORDS

This chapter will make it simple and easy for you to find the proper words to use in your writing. Whether you are writing emails, blog posts, newsletters or sales letters, choosing the proper words is important to the integrity of your product. Oftentimes, a query letter or marketing copy is the first representation of you and your work. Make it count!

The following word lists will make your writing dynamic, save you valuable time, and enhance your 'brand'.

APPEALING WORDS

- Exquisite
- Engaging
- Charming
- Pleasing
- Lovely
- Captivating

YOUR WORK IS AUTHENTIC WORDS

- Genuine
- Original
- One of a Kind
- Unique
- Real

WORDS SHOWING YOU ARE THE EXPERT

- Imagination
- Craftsmanship
- Seasoned
- Artistry
- Master
- Professional
- Better
- Talent

- Ingenious
- Capable
- Accomplished

- Expertly Trained
- Gifted

WORDS THAT SAY HONESTY

- Reputable
- Sincere
- Open
- Forthright
- Truthful
- Upfront

- Reliable
- Direct
- Revealing
- Candid
- Honest
- Frank

WORDS THAT CONVEY SAVING MONEY

- Cost efficient
- Bargain
- Money-saving
- World class
- Economical
- Best bet
- Affordable

- First class
- A value
- Safe Extra value
- Value pack
- Thrifty Bargain
- Inexpensive

WORDS THAT CREATE VALUE

- Crucial
- Prime
- Prerequisite
- Invaluable
- Vital

- Significant
- Indispensable
- Necessity
- Foundation

WORDS THAT WILL STIMULATE

- Gripping
- Compelling
- Imaginative
- Intoxicating
- Astounding
- Dynamic
- Bold
- Revealing
- Mesmerizing
- Thrilling
- Overwhelming
- Tempting
- Story
- Striking
- Vibrant
- Provocative
- New role
- Arresting
- Sensational
- Provoking
- Explosive
- Intriguing
- Tantalizing
- Alluring
- Fast Live it
- Vivid
- Amusing
- Lively
- Captivating
- Brilliant
- Titillating
- Inclusive
- Fascinating

WORDS THAT ARE APPEALING

- Irresistible
- Luscious
- Alluring
- Engaging
- Satisfy
- Pleasing
- Inviting
- Captivating
- Poignant
- Unforgettable

PERSONAL ACTION WORDS

<table>
<tr><td>

- Able
- Adaptable
- Ambitious
- Achiever
- Adept
- Bold
- Bright
- Capable
- Carrie
- Compassionate
- Confident
- Creative
- Dedicated
- Dependable
- Detail oriented
- Dynamic
- Eager
- Educated
- Efficient
- Energetic
- Enthusiastic
- Expert
- Experienced
- Flexible
- Focused
- Formidable
- Goal oriented
- Good listener
- Hard-working

</td><td>

- Highly motivated
- Honest
- Imaginative
- Industrious
- Ingenious
- Innovative
- Intelligent
- Judicious
- Likable
- Literate
- Lucy
- Managerial
- Motivated
- Multi-Talented
- Negotiator
- Open mind
- Organized
- Outgoing
- Out-of-the-box
- Passionate
- Patient
- Personable
- Polished
- Positive
- Productive
- Professional
- Proficient
- Qualified
- Quick thinking

</td></tr>
</table>

- Ready
- Reliable
- Resourceful
- Respected
- Seasoned
- Self-assured
- Serious
- Shrewd
- Skilled
- Smart
- Solid
- Sound
- Spirited
- Stable
- Straight shooting
- Successful
- Tactful
- Talented
- Team player
- Tenacious
- Top
- Trained
- Trustworthy
- Upbeat
- Valuable
- Versatile
- Veteran
- Well-Schooled
- Well-educated
- Willing
- Worldly
- World class

WORDS THAT CREATE VALUE

- Important
- Invaluable
- Essential
- Integral
- Vital
- Worthy
- Necessary
- Cherished
- Precious
- Irreplaceable
- Limited edition
- Wise investment
- Treasurers
- Matchless
- Upscale
- Precious commodity
- Exquisite

WORDS THAT DESCRIBE YOUR PRODUCT AS SUPERIOR

- Better
- Outstanding
- Superb
- Exceptional
- Excellent
- Distinguished
- Brilliant
- Unparalleled Class
- Excels
- Premium
- Ultimate
- Impeccable
- Flawless
- Finest
- Leading
- Tops
- Unmatched
- Unequal
- Unbeatable
- Surpasses
- Outshines
- Out-ranks
- Leading

MORE POWER WORDS

Without a doubt, you will hear the words below during your local newscast and even more so when watching national news. Because they are emotional words, they grab you, shake you, and get right in your face.

Journalists use the fear emotion, which is the most powerful emotion to get people's attention. With the highlighting of fear in their information, people are more likely to pay attention.

Network News does not want you to change the channel, so their scripts are loaded with fear words, making you worry you might miss something important. It is effective. Granted, you can overdo it, but in my opinion, most writers do not use these types of words enough. Words like these do connect with people and are serious attention grabbers. They also tap into the dramatic.

POWERFUL AND EMOTIONAL WORDS

- Agony
- Apocalypse
- Armageddon
- Assault
- Backlash
- Beating
- Beware
- Blinded
- Blindsided
- Blood
- Bloodbath
- Blood Curdling
- Bloody
- Bomb
- Buffoon
- Bumbling
- Cadaver
- Catastrophe
- Caution
- Collapse
- Corpse
- Crazy
- Cripple
- Crisis
- Danger
- Dangerously
- Deadly
- Death
- Destroy
- Devastating
- Disastrous
- Drowning
- Dumb
- Embarrass
- Fail
- Feeble
- Fired
- Fool
- Fooled
- Frantic
- Frightening
- Gambling
- Gullible
- Hack
- Hazardous
- Hoax
- Holocaust
- Horrific
- Hurricane
- Insidious
- Invasion
- IRS
- Jail
- Jeopardy
- Lawsuit
- Looming
- Lunatic
- Lurking

- Meltdown
- Mired
- Mistake
- Murder
- Nightmare
- Painful
- Pale
- Panic
- Peril
- Piranha
- Pitfall
- Plague
- Played
- Plummet
- Plunge
- Poison
- Poisoned
- Pummel
- Poor
- Prison
- Pus
- Reckoning
- Refugee
- Revenge
- Risky
- Scary
- Scream
- Searing
- Shatter
- Shellacking
- Silly
- Slaughter
- Slave
- Smash
- Strangle
- Stupid
- Suck
- Tailspin
- Tank
- Targeted
- Teetering
- Terror
- Terrorist
- Toxic
- Trap
- Vaporize
- Victim
- Volatile
- Vulnerable
- Warning
- Worry
- Wounded

Watch your local newscast tonight and see how many of these words in their scripts. Then watch, CNN or the National news and you will see that the newscast is written around types of words to keep viewers. It is similar to human behavior when people can't turn away from a car accident.

MOTIVATING YOUR READERS

Let's face it. When they're reading, most people are not exactly energetic. They are probably bored, maybe a little depressed, and usually tired. People love to be surprised. Anything that will wake them up or make them feel better is motivating their interest.

The good news?

Your writing can do that for them.

Use these power words to your reader excited and get them charged up again:

POWER WORDS THAT CREATE EXCITEMENT

- Amazing
- Audacity
- Backbone
- Belief
- Blissful
- Bravery
- Breathtaking
- Cheer
- Conquer
- Courage
- Daring
- Defiance
- Delight
- Devoted
- Excited
- Eye-opening
- Faith
- Fearless
- Fulfill
- Grateful
- Grit
- Guts
- Happy
- Heart
- Hero
- Hope
- Jaw-dropping
- Jubilant
- Magic
- Mind-blowing

- Miracle
- Pluck
- Sensational
- Spectacular
- Splendid
- Spirit
- Staggering
- Stunning
- Surprising
- Triumph
- Uplifting
- Valor
- Victory
- Wonderful
- Wondrous

WORDS THAT REVEAL

- Brazen
- Crave
- Depraved
- Dirty
- Exposed
- Forbidden
- Hypnotic
- Lascivious
- Lick
- Lonely
- Lust
- Naked
- Naughty
- Provocative
- Scandalous
- Sensual
- Sex
- Shameless
- Sinful
- Sleazy
- Spank
- Steamy
- Sweaty
- Tantalizing
- Tawdry
- Thrilling
- Uncensored
- Wanting
- Whip

INSTIGATING OTHERS

When creating art and especially when writing marketing copy, your job is to instigate others to take action. Unfortunately, business or marketing copy can be a little boring and most people are so inundated with advertisements, that they become apathetic. Your job is to spark interest from the onset and fan the flames. By using the power words below, you can connect with a consumer emotionally and play on those emotions to sustain their interest and ultimately make a sale.

WORDS THAT IGNITE

- Abuse
- Arrogant
- Backstabbing
- Beat-down
- Bully
- Coward
- Crooked
- Crush
- Disgusting
- Evil
- Force-fed
- Foul
- Hate
- Know-it-all
- Lies
- Loathsome
- Loser
- Lying
- Money-grubbing
- Nazi
- No Good
- Obnoxious
- Payback Pound
- Preposterous
- Punish
- Revolting
- Ruthless
- Sick and Tired
- Smug
- Sniveling
- Snob
- Snooty
- Snotty
- Stuck up
- Underhanded

STIMULATE THEIR GREED

Skim through good sales copy and you will find many of these power words. Many of them are so overused they have become cliché, but that does not inhibit them from working. The truth is, nearly everyone is interested in either making or saving money.

WORDS THAT TAP INTO DESIRES

- Bargain
- Best
- Billion
- Bonanza
- Cash
- Cheap
- Discount
- Dollar
- Double
- Explode
- Extra
- Feast
- Fortune
- Free
- Freebie
- Frenzy
- Frugal
- Gift
- Greatest
- Inexpensive
- Jackpot
- Luxurious
- Marked down
- Massive Money
- Nest egg
- Pay zero
- Prize
- Profit
- Quadruple
- Reduced
- Rich
- Savings
- Six-figure
- Skyrocket
- Soaring
- Surge
- Treasure
- Triple
- Whopping

WORDS THAT MAKE YOU FEEL SAFE AND TRUSTED

Your job as a salesperson is to make the buyer feel good about their potential purchase. This type of persuasion draws on creating a feeling of safety: You want to convince that buyer that they are making a financially as well as spiritually—as esoteric as this may seem—sound decision.

People want to be able to trust others. They need to trust both you and your product or service. They need to have confidence that you will deliver. Of course, building that kind of trust starts with a solid product, a quality brand and a credible reputation. Therefore, the words you use to describe yourself and your product very much matter. To help your customers feel safe, try using as many of these power words as possible:

- Anonymous
- Authentic
- Backed
- Best-selling
- Cancel Anytime
- Certified
- Endorsed
- Guaranteed
- Ironclad
- Lifetime Money Back
- No Obligation
- No Questions Asked
- No Risk
- No Strings Attached
- Official
- Privacy
- Protected
- Proven
- Recession-Proof Refund
- Research
- Results
- Secure
- Tested
- Try Before You Buy
- Verify
- Unconditional

TEASE THEM WITH THE FORBIDDEN FRUIT

Youth is synonymous with rebellion. The moment an adult told you not to do something, you immediately did the opposite. You were forbidden to do something and in trying to assert your autonomy, rebelled to rid yourself of stricture. This youthful feeling carries over into adult life, but it is buried under obligation and practicality. A good way to incite a consumer is to draw on this innate sense of rebellion.

The truth is, we are all fascinated by the mysterious and forbidden. Humans are curious by nature; we are all programmed that way. Whenever you need to create curiosity, sprinkle these power words throughout your writing, and readers cannot help being intrigued:

WORDS LIKE:

- Backdoor
- Banned
- Banished
- Behind the Scenes
- Black Market
- Blacklisted
- Bootleg
- Censored
- Concealed
- Confessions
- Confidential
- Controversial
- Covert
- Cover-up
- Forbidden
- Forgotten
- Hidden
- Illegal
- Insider
- Lost
- Off-limits
- Outlawed
- Private
- Secrets
- Smuggled
- Strange
- Unauthorized
- Withheld

POWERFUL PHRASES

Along with emotive words, there are powerful, emotive phrases as well. Powerful phrases identify a desire in the consumer and are characterized by their persuasiveness and immediacy. Use these phrases to make a big difference in your marketing copy and sales letters.

- Quick, simple, affordable
- You are looking for immediate results
- Save time; save money
- Enjoy in your home or in your car
- A benefit: this will save you time and money
- The design you won't forget
- Buy direct and save

- Captain your own ship
- Change your life forever
- Don't be left behind
- Don't miss the boat
- Dominate your field
- Once-in-a-lifetime opportunity
- Head-and-shoulders above the rest
- Hassle-Free
- Participation is limited
- An exclusive club
- Stand out from the crowd
- Shape your own tomorrow
- Sure to fit your budget
- Nothing- like it around
- Best value for the dollar
- A winning offer
- Find the answer to your problem
- Get results fast
- Helping smart business people like you
- Improve your bottom line
- Great incentives for buying
- Master your destiny
- Simplify your life

USING A SLOGAN FOR YOUR BUSINESS

Slogans are used for enhancing sales by triggering an emotion. In a slogan, verbs and adjectives are usually persuasive and nouns are clear and often repeated. A memorable slogan is concise, has a certain rhythm, and is under ten words. Slogans can help the consumer recall your product much faster. A slogan also makes your product much easier to identify. You will find slogans being used in larger corporations with astronomic marketing budgets. That said, using power phrases can be just as effective on a smaller scale. You will need to invest time to construct a slogan that will work specifically for you and your product.

MAKING YOUR SLOGAN MEMORABLE

- Make it thrilling

- Make an outrageous statement

- Use humor

- Make it inspirational

- Use dramatic language

The slogan is a powerful tool if constructed properly. All the major corporations use slogans that represent their company and product in marketing material such as print ads and television commercials. Let's look at some samples:

POPULAR CORPORATE SLOGANS

- Mercedes-Benz: The best or nothing

- Toyota: Let's go places

- Holiday Inn: Pleasing people the world over

- Nikon: At the heart of the image

- PlayStation: Live in your world, play in ours

- Energizer: That's positive energy

- Intel: Intel inside

- American Express: Don't leave home without it

- General Electric: We bring good things to life

- Avis: We try harder

- Ebay: Buy it. Sell it. Love it.

- L'Oreal: Because you're worth it

- LG: Life's good

- Sony: Make. Believe

- BMW: The ultimate driving machine

- Nokia: Connecting people

- Nike: Just do it
- Hallmark: When you care enough to send the very best
- McDonald's: I'm lovin' it
- KFC: Finger lickin' good
- IBM: THINK
- Visa: It's everywhere you want to be
- Panasonic: Ideas for life
- Lego: Play on
- Apple: Think different
- M&M- Melt in your mouth, not in your hand
- Campbell Soup- M'm m'm good!
- Coca-Cola: Life begins here (2011)
- Maxwell House: Good to the last drop
- Wheaties: Breakfast of champions
- Tide: Tide's in, Dirt's out
- Bounty: The quicker picker-upper
- HBO: It's not TV, it's HBO
- DeBeers: A diamond is forever
- Sharp: Sharp minds, sharp products
- Yahoo: Do you Yahoo?
- Rolaids: How do you spell relief?
- Burger King: Have it your way
- Timex: Takes a licking and keeps on ticking
- Clairol: Does she…or doesn't she?

The list goes on and on, but as you can see, these phrases are very familiar. This is the mark of an effective slogan. Should you choose to use a slogan, take your time and generate one that relates to your product and leaves a clear, lasting impression.

WRITING TO SELL

WRITING TO INFLUENCE

Artists commonly go through periods when it feels like no one is interested in their work. Mailers, letters, emails, postcards, flyers… you may as well open a window and throw all these papers into the wind for all the good they're doing. You might think: I am not getting the attention that I expected. Is it me? It is my work? This happens to all business owners, but artists seem to be more negatively affected by these times of uncertainly as their 'product' is deeply personal. When these publications seem to fail, it is time to shift the focus to emotive writing.

Being able to change and adapt your sales and marketing approach is crucial to your survival. Things change, people change, markets change. It is a fact that the majority of purchasing judgments derive from an emotion: For example, picture a balding man standing in the health/cosmetic section of a store. One product calls out to him: Regain the hair of your youth! This man is struck with a longing to grow his hair back: the product triggered this desire in him because he wants to regain the hair he had when he was younger because youth is synonymous with attractiveness. Thus, the hair product tapped into the man's desire to appear more attractive.

Your sales letter or marketing copy should reveal these emotive "hot-buttons". Push them! And persuade the consumer to buy.

There are two primary motivations that are important to remember:

1. The promise of gain
2. The fear of loss

The best time to reevaluate with these two motivations in mind is when you see your business slowing down. You must be aware of when and how to tap into these vital emotions. Put yourself in your consumer's perspective. Figure out their desires and, mostly importantly, empathize. This is especially true when considering how to market artwork. Because art is not always practical—indeed its very existence negates practicality—you need to identify an emotive void in your consumer that only your work can fill. Assure the consumer that their desire is common (drawing on the feeling of safety again) and that your product or artwork can fulfill their desire or alleviate their problem. In essence, your work will be their solution.

Be a grand storyteller. Tell your potential customer how you have encountered desires like theirs and have fulfilled such desires in the past. This is where having real testimonials is key. Testimonials are reputable people who explain their personal stories of an encounter with your product and how it benefitted them.

Stay focused on the emotive elements of the desire, not the facts or numbers. The consumer's emotional void is real and you, as the artist, can heroically help them out of their own funk.

1. Use powerful positive words and phrases that identify specific desires and emotions.
2. Empathize and create safety.
3. Reassure them that your work will certainly help them.

The emotional pitch is a tried and true option. However, there are times when instigating an emotional connection does not work. It could be that your product is just not attractive to the consumer. You might find yourself in a stagnating slump. Moments like these are when you begin to question your skills and talents. I can say honestly that even after being in this business as long as I have, I still have days like that.

You have to stop and re-evaluate yourself and your product:

1. Is my price too high?
2. Is my pitch professional?
3. Is my material top notch?
4. Is my market too 'soft'? I.e. are there too many sellers and not enough buyers in my market?
5. Is my product as good as I think it is?

When you reach this point, it's time to stop, regroup, step back and assess the big picture.

1. Is your letter written correctly and concisely?
2. Do you have power phrases or do you include negative or weak words in your sales letters/marketing copy?
3. Is your presentation professional? Or does it look amateur?

Based on my own experience of these uncertainties, I have found that it's usually a combination of things that slow down productivity and sales. Some things you can control, like your website, writing, and marketing materials. Some things are out of your control, like the economy, seasonal interest, or saturation of market. Look at the things you can control because it's no use sweating the things you can't control. Let's tackle writing quality, catchy letters and emails.

Here are words that can be psychologically detrimental for business correspondence:

Avoid using these words:

1. Buy - Never ask them to buy, purchase or invest.
2. Learn - People don't want to be told they have to learn. They will not learn from you, but they will become unconsciously educated about you and your work.
3. Tell - People don't like to be told. Make suggestions and the consumer will think it was their idea in the first place.

Let's look at an example. Examine these two lines:

1. Let me tell you how to lose weight in a week!
2. Let me disclose to you the secret of losing weight!

The second sentence is far more appealing. Why? Because you are suggesting that you have a solution to help them lose weight and the consumer is unconsciously deciding that your product might help them lose weight. It is an illusion, but an important psychological illusion.

Two more words to avoid:

1. Thing - 'Thing' is a very dull, ambiguous word to use. Tips, tricks, or techniques are much better options. Remember to use concrete terms.
2. Stuff - Stuff is a lazy, unprofessional word and shows no creativity. Be specific, what 'stuff'?

Yes, sometimes these words are used in marketing. However, your sales letter will stand out amongst this vagueness by using proper construction and powerful words and phrases. A sales letter has to be written with logic in mind, not just thrown together. Appraise your words and sentences carefully. Put each word on trial for its life. Use proper grammar and concrete terms as well.

HONESTY IN MARKETING

You always want to be honest, not misleading. Never make a promise that you don't intend to keep! For example, telling the consumer that your product will make them an instant millionaire is a potential business and public relations nightmare. The larger the promise, the more people's bullshit meter rises!

While it's true that salespeople are, by nature, bull-shitters, you are not a salesperson! There is no reason to make false promises to a potential customer. You are delivering a creative product that you made in exchange for its true value, no more and no less.

Because you have to market and sell using the written word, you have to take care in how you express, how you draft a letter, and the words you choose therein. A sloppy, misspelled letter or email will destroy any chances of success.

CREATING RAPPORT WITH YOUR WRITING

Your goal is to make every potential customer you meet feel a connection with you and your work. You want establish a trusting relationship between you and your client. Rapport is the ability to build credibility and is akin to reputation. Start building a trustworthy rapport in your initial marketing and sales writing. In your sales letter, it's prudent to include a few statements that have definite 'yes' answers.

EXAMPLES:

1. You realize how significant this is for you, don't you?
2. Don't you deserve the very best?
3. Isn't this the best time to start?
4. Won't building your business make you happy?
5. Wouldn't it be nice to afford that trip to Europe?

Using affirmative questions makes the potential buyer agree with you and begin to build trust. Once they agree with you, they forge a bond. They understand what you are saying and, in turn, they subconsciously think that this person thinks like I do. Establishing agreement also taps into the comfort and safety feeling discussed earlier.

In this modern era, everyone is a consumer. Therefore, everyone has experienced examples of trust and agreement in marketing. Let me provide a short anecdote: You are at a party and someone gets into a heated debate with you about politics. The conflict usually starts out with you versus them. If you're like me, you make some outrageous statement, sometimes just to surprise and get everyone's attention. You usually go it alone at first, however, how cool do you feel when a couple of your friends take your view and join in on the conversation? You become empowered. You feel supported. Your friends have come to your aide. This is probably a scenario, which you have experienced. It works the same way when dealing with a stranger or consumer. A closeness and feeling of kinship is shared when two people agree or share the same view. The way to achieve this is by using those affirmative 'YES' questions.

CREATING RAPPORT THROUGH MIRRORING

Mirroring – a marketing term denoting a technique used to establish rapport with a person

Mirroring is a behavior in which one person copies or assumes the characteristics of another person. This technique can be used in writings, by understanding and empathizing with a consumer perspective. Yet, it can also be used in social interactions, such as meetings, gallery openings, gala events or industry dinners. You probably already practice mirroring in social situations without realizing it. The practice may include copying gestures, movements, language, accents, tones, tics, expressions, eye movement, and breathing. In general, people usually accept their mirror image. I'm not suggesting a robotic replication or a theater arts exercise, but a subtle awareness of how another person operates. Mirroring the person you are in conversation with can make them feel more relaxed and encourages them to open up.

Anthropologically, humans notably react favorably to and place faith in those who are like them, who think and speak like they do. Mirroring is a practice that taps into this truth.

MIRRORING TECHNIQUES

1. Use similar body language.
2. Slow or speed up your speech pattern to match theirs.
3. Use the similar words and word patterns.
4. Mimic body and hand movements.

NEURO-LINGUISTIC PROGRAMMING (NLP)

Years ago, I studied Neuro-Linguistic Programming (NLP), which supplies a theory that neurological, linguistic and cognitive patterns are intrinsically connected. NLP is used to stimulate a particular behavior from an individual. Many motivational speakers of today use some element of NLP to persuade people to change their thinking.

NLP is a set of solution-oriented attitudes and beliefs (NLP Presuppositions). The presuppositions are beliefs that guide the development of NLP. They are not necessarily valid, but sometimes produce useful results. Beliefs are usually self-fulfilling. In effect, if we believe someone doesn't like us, our defensive manner can make this a reality. They are called presuppositions because you presuppose them to be true and then act as if they are. If you like the results, then continue to act as if they are right. These results form a set of ethical principles for life. NLP is very interesting reading. Some of the beliefs of NLP are:

1. The meaning of any communication is the response it elicits.
2. There are no failures in communication, only outcomes and feedback.
3. The map (set of beliefs) is not the territory (reality).
4. Every person lives in accordance with his or her own unique model of the world.
5. People always make the best choices available to them, given their unique model of the world and of the situation.
6. People have all the resources necessary to make any desired change.
7. There is no substitute for clean, open sensory channels.
8. If what you are doing is not working, do something different.
9. In-group interactions, the person with the most flexibility and behavioral options will control the outcome of the interaction.
10. An individual's worth is held as positive and constant, whereas the value and appropriateness of their internal and/or external behavior is open to question.

MODELING

Develop your model by emulating the processes of others who achieved success by your standards; tweak this model so it is personal to you. From that modeling process, a whole host of interesting and useful techniques have evolved. Specifically, some people tend to process information more visually, while others absorb through auditory faculties, and still others process via kinesthetic, i.e. doing. Educators have used these models to develop methods to teach children according to what is most 'natural' for each specific child.

In summary, NLP starts with a singular, powerful premise: There is always a way to achieve a goal, despite any methods or techniques attempted in the past. Becoming familiar with the psychology of NLP and its principles may greatly increase your effectiveness in sales and marketing by revealing new and innovative ways to reach people in a variety of environments.

COMMON WRITING FLUBS

Let's face it: there are a thousand ways to lose a sale. While there is no exact science to determine why you lose a sale, your sale letters should not count among the reasons. Your product, your marketing angle and your sales letter are all within your control. Particularly in your sales letter, you decide which information to include and the manner in which it is delivered. It all starts with quality writing.

Keep in mind that you are using a sales letter and marketing package in place of sending out a physical salesperson like larger corporations do. Large corporations have large budgets for sales and marketing and therefore have far more resources at their disposal. The reality of small business, especially in the art world, is that you have to work harder and be smarter to make up for the lack of resources. Unlike a salesperson, your letter cannot overcome objections quickly. This means that your letter must avoid any and all mistakes that many sales letters contain. In the end, however, the goal and success of a salesperson or well-crafted sales letter is the same: secure a sale. So, it's imperative that you convince the reader effectively in your letter to buy your work, attend your event (to buy your work), etc.....

SIMPLICITY

The most common mistake in letter writing is distracting the reader with confusing or indirect language. Too much information is far worse than too little information. You want to get it right in the middle, with just enough information to interest the reader and induce them to seek out more information (this is where good contact information is important). However, simplicity is key. Here is a good acronym to help you remember:

1. K - Keep
2. I - It
3. S - Simple
4. S - Stupid

Keep your letter focused on a central message. A ten-page sales letters will most likely NEVER be read all the way through. Get-in and get-out with your message intact. It's a good idea to write a simple thesis statement and consistently refer to it while you're drafting your letter. For example, the objective of my sales letter might be to convince art lovers to come to my gallery opening. If this is the objective, then my thesis would look something like: If you love art, please come to my gallery opening at ———— on ————. The rest of your letter should support, in logical steps, this central theme.

KEEP IT INTERESTING

While keeping simplicity in mind, you don't want to restrict yourself in your sales letter either. As in all things, the key is balance. Write everything you need to write to get the objective across, yet write it creatively and with concision.

FOUR MAJOR ELEMENTS OF AN INTERESTING LETTER

1. Reinforce your expertise. Give concrete reasons why you are the expert.
2. Illuminate the benefits of working with you.
3. Evaluate desires, fears and doubts with pinpoint questions. Get inside the reader's head!
4. Ask them to act NOW on your offer.

Keeping your letter and all of your writing for that matter laser focused and having no irrelevant or confusing information is the key to keep the reader interested.

Another thing you will want to do is add flair to your writing, so your writing won't be boring and dry. Using power words and phrases and colorful statements will help you do this. Your writing needs to sound interesting and exciting. For example you have to nice product you have an amazing product.

THE SALES LETTER

WHY WRITE A SALES LETTER?

Sales letters are an imperative step in the sales and marketing process. While hard-copy letters sent via snail-mail are becoming a bit obsolete, emails and online mailing lists are certainly a handy and readily used tool in a salesperson's kit. Sales letters function in many useful ways: They reach a broader audience on a personal level than you ever could on foot. Can you outrun a fiber optic cable? Didn't think so. Secondly, they communicate more information than a simple ad or flyer. And finally, they do some of the vetting process before you spend the time and energy to meet with a potential client. If a person responds to a sales letter, you know they have at least a modicum of interest in your work and you can spend that in-person time discussing specifics and not giving a general pitch. However, don't be lulled into thinking that a letter will make your phones ring off the hook with orders. It will merely open the door and it's up to you to step inside and prove to a potential client why you are the right choice. First thing's first, though: Let's open the door to a broad and varied sales base!

DEFINING THE SALES LETTER

Sales Letter - A well-written piece of correspondence designed to attraction attention and to influence others to purchase your product or service.

The main objectives of a sales letter are…

1.　To sell yourself or your art,
2.　To notify everyone about your objectives as an artist,
3.　And to generate interest with your work to potential buyers.

Anyone can write a good sales letter but it takes practice to write a great one!

Before writing a sales letter, you—the writer— must put yourself in the reader's shoes. This is the foundation of marketing in general. You must learn to think like your customer, i.e. your target-marketing group. This will be discussed in-depth later. To begin, ask yourself these questions:

1. How do you feel when you are pitched or preached to?

2. What kind of marketing correspondence grabs your attention? How can you reproduce this so it is specific to your product?

3. Do you read any of the sales letters you get? Why or why not?

4. What makes some letters more interesting than others?

Unfortunately, most sales letters end up in the trash. Most people view sales letters as a waste of their time. Many letters are poorly written, fail to accurately represent a professional image, and contain extraneous and confusing information. Effective sales letters are accurate, professional and well written.

Remember, you are showcasing your art as well as yourself. Make a great first impression!

ALWAYS INCLUDE THESE ELEMENTS:

1. A concise, accurate description of your product/service

2. Benefits for buying your product/service

3. Reasons why your product/service is unique

GOOD QUESTIONS TO ASK BEFORE YOU BEGIN:

1. What advertising mediums will you use? Internet, TV, Radio, Print

2. What benefits does your product offer?

3. DO you have supporting sales material such as brochures, pamphlets, websites, and videos?

4. Who is your direct competition?

5. How does your competition market?

6. Do you have an advertising budget?

7. Who are your potential clients?

8. What would make someone buy your product?

WRITING STRATEGY

Advertising copywriters follow a model with the acronym: A.I.D.A

- A   Attention
- I   Interest
- D   Desire
- A   Action

ATTENTION

The goal is to get your readers' attention, which is no easy task. This can be done in two ways:

1. A hard-hitting headline
2. Powerful lead paragraph

Examples: Do you want to cut your electricity costs by 40%?

What if we could help you lose 20 pounds in 3 weeks?

These headlines answer the reader's principle question: "What do I gain?" By letting the reader know right off the bat that they can gain from your letter, odds are that they will continue to read. You have successfully grabbed their attention!

INTEREST

Next, you must hold their interest. You have to show the reader why they need your product or service. Why do you think your product makes their life better or easier, or in some way make them happier? Create a scenario in their mind where they are missing out without your work. The best way to make others feel like they are missing out is with the use of testimonials from satisfied past customers. Or, if applicable, generate a list of prominent people in the community who have purchased your artwork: Doctors, lawyers, art dealers, politicians, police or firemen, judges and celebrities. An endorsement from this kind of clientele will (unfortunately or not) establish your worth. By having satisfied clients, you have gained instant credibility by letting them know others have made their life better by purchasing your work.

DESIRE

Create a desire or demand for your work. First, you need to identify potential desires your customer might have. To do this, you must link your work to positive associations. Positive associations include things like how others love your work or how your work solved a problem for them. Cultivate satisfaction!

Examples:

Weight-loss products that show attractive, happy people on vacation with a beautiful island in the background. The desire established here is for the customer to see him/herself on the beach in a well-fitting swimsuit, good body, and arm around a loved one. This creates a happy thought that will induce desire.

Male enhancement products that show older people dancing, smiling, cuddling, all because of this miracle pill!

ACTION

Taking action is exactly what it sounds like. What do you want the reader to do next? Buy your product! Motivate them to be proactive. Schedule a meeting or have them meet you for coffee— you need them to get in contact with you so you can show them you're as good as you say.

SALES LETTER FUNDAMENTALS:
THE 12-STEP PROGRAM

1. Demand attention with your heading.
2. Identify needs, wants, and/or problems.
3. Provide a way to satisfy or solve. Become their savior!

4. Present your skill set.

5. Highlight the benefits of your product.

6. Prove your credibility by providing references and testimonials that solidify any claims you have made.

7. Make a final offer on an attractive package deal, bonus or discount. Give them a lucrative deal that most wouldn't refuse.

8. Guarantee your client. Guarantees solidify the deal, elevate trust and eliminate risk factors.

9. Create urgency by suggesting scarcity. I.e., your offer won't last forever. Stimulate action by reminding them that this is an exclusive, limited offer.

10. Call to action: Provide easy contact information or ordering details. Ex: "one-click" purchases, toll-free numbers that deliver a product simply and quickly.

11. Remind them that your work is available on a first come, first serve basis. Put the risk of loss on the table if they don't take action now.

12. Add a Postscript (P.S.). Close with a reminder summarizing a special or offer or some other interesting nugget of information. Postscripts can be a very effective tool.

Letters that stand out include:

- Name and logo on your letterhead
- Catchy and creative headlines: Sometimes these clinchers grab attention well in BOLD, italic or red lettering
- A real signature at the bottom of the letter
- Sub-headlines that logically flow from the headline
- Testimonials from clients that own your work or used your service and loved it.
- Simple order and payment methods
- Persuasive "Call to Action"
- Conversational, yet polished language
- Correct grammar
- Humor
- Emotive language

COMPONENTS OF A SALES LETTER

1. Headline
2. Lead paragraph
3. Body
4. Closing

HEADLINE

The headline is the first bit of writing that your reader will see. Therefore, it has to be the sharpest, most interesting statement you can make. Stimulate an emotional reaction and create a bond with the reader right from the onset.

Let's take a diet and weight loss product for example. A poor headline might read:

Are you concerned that you will become fat and unattractive?

While a headline in the form of a question is a good tactic, this example does not stimulate any emotion other than making the reader feel bad about themselves. This is absolutely the opposite reaction you would want to illicit from your reader. A better question to ask is:

- Do you want to lose 20 LBS in three weeks?
- OR, in statement form:

We can show you how to lose 20 LBS in three weeks!

With the latter two headlines, you:

Involve the reader personally

Identify a desire

Illicit an emotion

Induce them to keep keeping

When these four elements work simultaneously, this is the indication of a good headline.

TYPES OF HEADLINES

1. **DISCOVERY:** This headline 'discovers' a feeling or emotion. It illuminates a want or desire that the reader may or may not have realized they had before. A good discovery headline persuades the reader that they have this desire and should seek to fulfill it.

EXAMPLES:

We can show you how to make a livable salary by working from home.

Discover the inside tips that turned amateur golfers into pros!

The first headline identifies two desires:

- Making a living and.
- Working from home.

If the reader identifies with these two common desires, then they will respond and keep reading. In the second headline, the identified desires are:

- Improving your golf game
- Impressing colleagues and friends with new skill, and
- Earning the prestige of playing golf like a professional.

2. **TESTIMONIAL:** Anchor your credibility to satisfied customers directly in your headline. A testimonial establishes trust between you and your reader.

EXAMPLES:

- I couldn't put the book down. It was a real page-turner!
- I learned more reading her book that I have in my ten years in the field.

Both of these headlines identify a desire to read an interesting and informative book. Testimonials, by design, identify a desire, assure satisfaction for that desire and provide a concrete example of such satisfaction.

3.   **COMMAND**: A command headline demands the reader to act and readily stimulates a desire to act.

EXAMPLES:

- Create a beautiful home.
- Take control of your finances.

Command headlines identify desires and stimulate emotion. They are also punchy, demanding and invigorating statements that involve the reader personally.

4.   **NEWS:** There is a reason why you continue reading the article below a newspaper headline. These headlines deliver interesting, scandalous and/or astonishing factual statements.

EXAMPLES:

If you liked the Salad Chopper 2.0, you'll love the Salad Chopper 3.0!

Now introducing: A new line of Graphic Tee designs from a visual artist you love. Usually, this type is used when introducing a new product/service or one that is improved.

5.   **Guarantee:** Everyone likes a sure thing. Provide a guarantee in your headline. Akin to testimonials, guarantees develop a trust between you and your reader. Share attractive benefits of your product and guarantee results.

EXAMPLES:

- My stunning chandeliers will make your home the envy of your neighbors.

- Commission a beautiful mural that takes no more than three days to complete!

6.   **QUESTION:** Ask a question in your headline that the reader will eagerly want to answer or have answered. Ask an affirmative question to which the reader will definitively answer, "Yes" or "No".

EXAMPLES:

- Do you want a beautiful garden retreat right in your urban apartment?
- Do you want to miss out on an exciting opportunity to support your local arts?

LEAD PARAGRAPH

Okay, so you've written your headline. The reader's attention is sufficiently grabbed. Good, now let's keep that attention by writing a killer lead paragraph. Begin by asking yourself these questions:

What is the ultimate goal I want to achieve with this letter?

A goal should be established so you can easily refer back when writing the body of your letter. Your goal functions in very much the same way a thesis statement would. Having a goal focuses your letter and disallows you from writing tangents and confusing your reader.

What subject or desire did I introduce in my headline?

By identifying the emotion and desire piqued in the headline, you carry that ember forward into the letter to fan the flame of interest. Remember, sub-headings must logically flow from headlines. The same is true about topic sentences and supporting sentences. Each component of the letter should follow similar logic.

What is the most important information I want to communicate to my reader?

Statistically speaking, a potential customer will not read more than a few sentences of your sales letter. Therefore, you must convey the most important, interesting information in the first few sentences of your letter. Think of it this way: If I only had two sentences to make a sales pitch, how would I do it? Use the answer you generate as your lead paragraph.

GUIDE THE READER

Write an attention-grabbing first sentence by implementing those buzz word lists. After the reader's interest is piqued with that first sentence or two, go into the particulars of your objective. Like in journalistic pieces, the first paragraph should always have the 5 W's:

1. WHO
2. WHAT
3. WHEN
4. WHERE
5. WHY

ADDITIONAL TIPS

Include interesting information and use strong, commanding language always begin in "First Person", i.e. I want to tell you about…

Never begin with weak, unconfident language: "I hope you find my work interesting." Instead say, "You will find my work interesting."

Target a specific audience

Keep it concise

Sentences must to be precise and sharp.

SAMPLES OF STRONG LEAD PARAGRAPHS

EXAMPLE 1:

Dear Mr. X,

Do you wish that you had a service that could maximize profits for your business?

If you answered 'yes', my consulting firm is just what you need to increase sales and profits for your business. Consider this the day your business takes a leap forward and gains an edge in your market.

EXAMPLE 2:

Dear Mrs. Y,

I know you're ready to take your business to the next level. Best business practice is all about increasing sales and maximizing profit. My consulting firm can achieve this for you. Skeptical? Allow me to convince you: I will work to increase your sales 10, 20, or even 30% by implementing a few ingenious techniques.

BODY

The body of your letter should not consist of more than 2-4 paragraphs. In fact, the entirety of your letter should not exceed 1 page in length. While keeping your initial goal in mind, the body should highlight the benefits of your product or service will offer. Additionally, the body is the section in which to include credentials, testimonials, special offers, package deals, and bonuses.

BENEFITS SELL, FEATURES DO NOT!

Again, benefits sell, features do not! The difference between benefits and features is to whom information about your product or service is accommodating. A list of features is merely accommodating your need to relay information. Therefore, it excludes the potential customer. Features are the equivalent of being talked at instead of having a conversation. A list of benefits on the other hand, center around the best interest of the client. Benefits include the reader and get them thinking directly about their own situation and how your product or service might accommodate them.

BONUSES

Everyone loves getting a good deal. Just by adding the word(s) "Bonus" or "Special Deal", it lends your sales pitch a measure of immediacy and value. A bonus can be anything that you offer that has more value than a regular sale. Suppose you teach piano lessons: An added bonus would be to offer two lessons for free if the customer signs up in the month of January. Other examples of added value include: an additional painting, custom frame, a custom jingle for their business, etc..... A bonus also personalizes and connects you to your customer. Everyone wants to feel special. Be sure to use a personal phrase like "Just for you!" to make that connection. Remember to keep your bonus simple; do not make a bonus difficult to send, deliver or receive. A bonus must also relate to your work not be something completely off base like housesitting or a trip to the zoo. Keep your bonus offers short and exact.

A bonus always has a value attached to it!

Additionally, be wary about what you choose to offer as a bonus. Your bonus should not be something that significantly reduces your profit margin. In fact, offering a ridiculously generous bonus actually makes you look desperate and achieves the opposite effect: it devalues and distracts from your main product.

A bonus is a great little tool to nudge a prospective client into making a purchase. It goes without saying that if you feel that you have the sale in hand, you don't need to offer any bonus. Hold that ace in the hole until a time when you need it.

GUARANTEES

Providing a guarantee is all about taking pride in what you do! Reassure your potential client that you are the expert. Guarantees are not-so-subtle messages that assure your customer that you are the real deal, that your product is genuine and that you are trustworthy.

THE WORLD IS FULL OF EXPERTS, JUST ASK THEM!

This all comes down to quality and frugality. You have to decide what your marketing angle will be. If your product is on the expensive side, stress in your guarantee that your product is worth the extra money, that your product has quality. Conversely, if your product is in direct competition with similar products, stress the lower cost of your product, but maintain the quality. If your buyer becomes convinced that they can get a better deal and better quality elsewhere, they will not buy from you. So, do your market research and develop a good, honest guarantee.

Emphasize that a guarantee can and will help them. There are so many scams and cons to take people's money. By being upfront, honest and prideful in your work, your guarantee will leave the buyer feeling more secure and trust working with you. Owning what you do and being responsible will make your client happy and facilitate repeat business. Do all you can to cultivate this.

TIPS ON OFFERING A GUARANTEE

- Live and do business by your philosophy.
- Make it easy and simple!
- Drop the fine print that keeps lawyers in business.
- React quickly and make good on your guarantee.
- Have a basic guarantee for general scenarios and tweak as situations arise.
- Note that some types of guarantees may not apply to your business at all.

Carefully craft your own guarantee.

GUARANTEE TYPES

"MONEY-BACK" GUARANTEE: Full refund? How long after the purchase?

"SATISFACTION "GUARANTEE: Do they get their money back if not satisfied? How long is the window of opportunity to report dissatisfaction? Since art is subjective, you may want to define satisfaction. Such as: Is the artwork defective? Damaged?

"PRICE" GUARANTEE: Is your work the least expensive? Do you want it to be?

"ON TIME" GUARANTEE: Are you late with delivery? I wouldn't set a time constraint to the creation of the product. As artists, it is in your nature to 'sit with' a project and you are also subject to creative blockages as well. However, if you agree to ship a product by a specific date/time: MEET THAT DEADLINE!

"NO QUESTIONS ASKED" GUARANTEE: Are there any exceptions to your guarantee? Be wary in return-policies and this guarantee. People will find any excuse to get their money back.

Guarantees are all personal decisions. Being an artist, you are creating something that is unique, not a mass-produced knock-off. You really have to think carefully about how you want to handle a guarantee. Yes, they are important, but where do you draw the line? A few years back, when I produced commercials, I was constantly in conflict with this very same question. I would get all the information from my client, understand their product and their message, and be sure to craft something that would satisfy all their demands. I would edit the spot together, send them the rough cut and they... HATE IT! What?

Before I knew any better, I can't tell you how many times I had to go back and re-edit spots until my client was completely satisfied. I would accommodate every little grievance: I didn't like the shirt I was wearing, or I looked to fat in that shot, or The shelf had the old product on it, or even I wanted my nephew in at the beginning! It all became a real pain in the butt, and mind you, I was shooting two and three commercials a week. So, I had to come up with a solution: I came up with an approval process: we generate a script, they sign off on the script, we show them the shots on the shoot and they sign off on those shots, etc.... Contact info, product in store, etc.... all had to be signed off on and approved before we completed a project. Therefore, we could guarantee satisfaction!

That little anecdote aside, the point is that YOU have to decide what you want to offer for a guarantee. Do you re-edit the spot because they had green shirt on and they didn't look good in green? You must set boundaries. Your time and energy spent should equal the profit. Only you can set your principles and stick to them.

SIMPLE GUARANTEE TAG LINES

1. 100% Risk-Free

2. Peace of mind

3. It doesn't get much better than this!

INSTANT GRATIFICATION

Building on the principle that your sales letter should be driven by emotion, there's no better way to illicit emotion than to deliver instant gratification:

1. Quick and easy transaction!
2. Free bonus with every order!
3. The most talked-about product in town!
4. Guaranteed satisfaction!
5. Great product support!
6. Free shipping and/or delivery!
7. We take credit cards!

HIGHLIGHTING YOUR PRODUCT/SERVICE

The most important element in the body of your sales letter is a thorough, yet concise description of the product or service you are offering. Accurately relay all the necessary information regarding your artwork. This might be a good place to include reviews or testimonials as well. Additionally in this section, briefly provide your credentials and personal history to make a connection with your reader. You may want to include projects you are currently working on or will be working on in the future. Make choices that are accurate, relevant and things you can deliver on.

CLOSING

Your closing statement is quite important. This is where you:

1. Induce them to take action and buy now!

2. Provide contact details.

TEST MARKETS

Always test out your letter on your friends and family to get input and feedback. A person, who knows you and your work, yet is not privy to the particulars of your sales approach will be the best trail run for your letter. If your friends and family are confused or find the letter boring, chances are a potential customer will be as well. No matter how small or insignificant a suggestion may sound, consider it carefully. And remember, don't take it personally. Letting your ego standing the way of valuable help will get you exactly nowhere.

All this is to say something vital:

ALWAYS HAVE A SECOND SET OF EYES READ YOUR WORK!

I'll rephrase to make sure it sticks:

NEVER SEND OUT WRITING THAT ONLY YOU HAVE EDITED!

Having someone else proofread your letter is always a good idea. Even the most seasoned writers overlook grammatical and mechanical mistakes. Get as many people to read your letter as possible. One can never have too many editors.

AVOID THESE COMMON MISTAKES

1. AVOID sending out blind bulk emails and/or mailers
2. AVOID long-winded letters
3. AVOID overly pretentious language; be professional, but conversational
4. AVOID bragging or long lists of credentials

The worst thing that can happen in a sales letter is for a potential customer to become turned off by your pitch and stop reading. Unfortunately, this happens all the time. I'm sure you get your share of spam from companies wanting your business, cluttered with facts that are useless to you, in a language you need a translator to understand. In fact, I recently ripped up a letter just like that from a life insurance company. I was looking for quotes for another policy and what I got was a letter that resembled the theory on Quantum Physics! I angrily and gladly chucked that one in the trash. Don't write a letter like this!

Keep personal information out of your letter. No one cares if your kid just took their first step or graduated from college. You can and should address that personal stuff face-to-face once you establish a relationship with your customer. However, the sales letter must immediately get down to business (pardon the pun). High-end sales professional told me that you have 10 seconds to grab someone's attention. 10 seconds! So, like a thoroughbred racehorse, you need to fly out of the gates with your best information.

Knowing this, you need to definitely write intelligently:

Design a sales letter that is just as much a work of art as your product. Write something that will make you stand out and become memorable.

WHAT GOES INTO A GOOD SALES LETTER?

10 Basic Rules for Writing a Good Sales Letter:

1. Always target needs and wants
2. Write to specific people not general mailboxes
3. Note that people buy benefits not features, i.e. saving money, improving their life, etc......
4. Hook the reader in your first line
5. Provide the reader with specific information
6. Use a conversational tone, that which imbues personality
7. Have others read your writing. Test it out on friends and family!
8. Keep your letter appropriate to your goals
9. Use good writing aesthetics, i.e. use basic fonts and letter-structure
10. Include clear information on how to order your product; include clear contact information.

Ok, now you have the basics. Let's bolster those basics with a few specific tips:

TIPS

- Always use your prospective client's name and title in your letter
- Make your letter user-friendly and comprehensive; avoid jargon
- Use slogans, phrases and catchy headlines
- Write like you speak while still maintaining proper grammar
- Keep paragraphs short and concise
- Write your letter, then put it away and come back to it for evaluation in a day or two: distance breeds perspective
- Get feedback from family and friends
- Use consistent format and structure in your letters and writing
- Add a postscript (P. S.) to attract attention
- Always use your BEST testimonials
- Make an irresistible offer
- Connect to your readers by tapping into emotions
- Always include a "Call to Action"
- Provide easy contact information (phone number, email, website); for example, include a business card
- Tell them where and how to order
- Keep your letter exciting, interesting and fun
- Always offer a guarantee of some sort
- Handwrite the address on the envelope for a personal touch
- Always follow up within a week

A well-crafted sales letter will absolutely help you in this business of art. When combined with effective networking and good old-fashioned hard work, sales letters will put you on a fast track to finding new clients.

ELEMENTS TO CONSIDER

HOPE: Create a sense of hope. An effective sales letter identifies needs/wants and offers the opportunity to satisfy them.

URGENCY: Create urgency to stimulate the reader into taking action now, i.e. ordering your product and/or contacting you for more information

AUTHORITY: You are the expert! You are the authority on your work. You know your art; you make it, live and breath it. Now, communicate this authority and passion to your potential customer.

UNBIASED: A customer can buy from you or not. They can buy from your competition. You will be professional either way.

FEAR PERSUADES: Tap into their emotions. Consumers are driven by a fear that they will miss out on a special product or deal. Make it clear that there are consequences to not buying from you. Identify that fear and then help them overcome it.

ORIGINALITY: Dare to be different! Your art is unique to you. Make your sales letter one of a kind as well.

EXERCISE:

Generate short answers to these pertinent questions. These answers will make good reference material on what to include in your sales letter.

- Who are your potential customers?
- What is your target group?
- What kind of people would like your work?
- What is unique about your work?
- What makes your work better than a competitor?
- What makes your work more attractive?
- What should someone purchase from you?
- What kind of credibility do you have?

- What benefits do you offer?

- What guarantees will you make?

- Do you have excellent service or quick delivery?

- What are some of the objections you may encounter?

- Is your work priced reasonably?

- Can my client get my quality for less money from a competitor?

- Why do you want the reader to act now?

- How will you motivate a customer to buy?

- Do you have any bonus offers or special deals?

- Do you have a limited time offer?

WHY YOU?

Rejection is hard. We have all dealt with it, whether in business or in personal life. Every salesperson has to deal with rejection too. There is no doubt that you will deal with, or have already dealt with objection to your work. A thirty-year veteran of cable advertising sales once told me that the more rejections you get the easier it is to get over them. So, while it may be more difficult to stomach rejection with your own artwork, you are the best person for the job. Here's why: You are your own best advocate. The key is to develop a tough outer shell and not take rejection too personally.

OVERCOMING OBJECTIONS

You will have to be prepared to answer the tough questions when pitching your product or service. One of the toughest questions is: "Why should I buy from you?" Be prepared to overcome that objection.

One technique that salespeople use is to take the offense, or using 'reverse psychology'. Instead of telling customers to buy from you, go the opposite direction. Make the sale by telling them to purchase from a competitor. How does this work? You are planting a seed of doubt. Sow this seed with an assumption that they will be dissatisfied. Tell them to contact you when that happens and you can help them out. Or, thank them for their time, express hope that the competitor will satisfy them. Punctuate this by saying something like, "If [competitor] doesn't satisfy you, I guess you'll be paying twice. Once for them and once for my product." Believe it or not, reverse psychology does work. However, I would not make a habit of doing this. The only time you would do this is when you're at the point where it doesn't look like you will get the sale. It's definitely worth a try.

Another way to avoid upfront objections is to write a sales letter that anticipates objections and surmounts them.

EXAMPLES OF CUSTOMER RESISTANCE

- "I really can't afford it now."
- "You work won't help me."
- "I don't believe your pitch."
- "What if I hate your work?"
- "Let me think about it."
- "That's very expensive."

The list goes on and on. There will always be excuses not to buy.

Pre-qualifying these people prior to investing your time is smart. Even then, however, people are fickle and change their minds. You have to prepare answers to their resistance and hesitation. As mentioned previously, YOU need to know what your product is and how it will benefit a potential customer. Spend ample time practicing all possible scenarios to spin the cost objection in your favor.

Overt rejections aside, remember that there are two major factors to get someone motivated:

THE POTENTIAL OF GAIN

Paint a mental picture for your customer. Vividly express how life will improve for them after owning a piece of your artwork or soliciting a service from you. For example, explain how purchasing from you will increase their status in the community by showing support for the local arts. Or, how your piece will make their office look hip and on the cutting edge, which in turn communicates how savvy their business is. Projecting the potential for GAIN will always get a buyer thinking positively and open the door to considering buying from you. You have free rein to spin it any way you want; just make them believe they will GAIN from this decision.

THE FEAR OF LOSS

The fear of loss is a very strong emotion. No one want to be a loser. Let your potential client know that they will lose something if they do not purchase from you. It might mean that they are not are trendy as they think they are. Or, that the person who does purchase your work will possess a one-of-a-kind piece of work. You might suggest that their business is worth being augmented by your work, that making smart decisions and thinking outside the box are the cornerstones of good business. Convince them that others who purchase from you put their business or home in a better position. You can even mention the hundreds of investors who passed on Google and Facebook when they were just start-up companies. How do those investors feel now that they passed on such a large opportunity? A simple 'fear' tagline would be something like:

Why wouldn't you enhance your business when you have the chance?

Or

We have inside information to help prevent you being laid off from your job.

These are no-brainers. The customer would read something like this; digest the suggestion that they are not as invaluable to their company as they thought. Then, they begin to think about joblessness, which in turn triggers worst-case scenarios: no job = no mortgage, car, insurance payments = no security. Conclusion: I need to purchase this service so I don't lose my job. While this may seem a bit ruthless, inducing fear works.

ADDITIONAL TIPS

- Keep a folder of well-written letters and ads you come across in your research and use them as templates
- Create a customer profile for each current and potential client; include up-to-date contact information

- Keep the 5 W's in mind: Who, What, When, Where, Why?

Remember, brevity is key. You want to provide the essential information. Any additional questions a customer might have will induce them to contact you.

FORMATTING

SALES LETTER FORMAT

An aesthetically pleasing letter isn't rocket science. Implement these suggestions.

Use a readable font, nothing fancy: Times New Roman is the standard, but Times, Courier, and Arial are also acceptable choices.

Format using 1.5" margins and either 1.5 or double spacing.

Use 11 or 12pt font, nothing smaller or larger.

Bold headers and bullet-points to make it eye-catching. If you want, use a different color (other than standard black) to emphasize a particularly interesting or important point. However, don't overdo color. Pick 1-3 colors that are complementary and not garish. You don't want a rainbow letter.

If you have a logo, use it in the upper left-hand header next to your name and contact information.

DO NOT use Clip Art or other stock imagery anywhere in your letter. This is tacky.

If you choose to include pictures of your work with mailers, be sure to spend the money on good photography and good quality printing. Pixelated, blurry and uninteresting pictures are a huge indicator of poor quality.

SALES LETTER SUMMARY

Your sales letter needs immediately answer the two big questions:

1.   Who you are.

2.   What you do.

Remember to include:

1.   Your logo on your letterhead
2.   Your name/business name
3.   Contact information: email, phone number, website, blog, etc.…

Last-Minute Reminders:

1.   Keep your sentences short.
2.   Use precise language.
3.   Put yourself in your customer's shoes.
4.   Identify a desire
5.   Satisfy that desire.
6.   Showcase your expertise.

LOOKING THE PART

PERSONAL APPEARANCE

Does appearance really matter? If you're an artist—and you probably are if you're reading this book—you already know the answer. Of course appearances matter. Aesthetics are very important. A large percentage of judgment happens when initially seeing a person. Therefore, it is vital that you give an excellent first impression. No t-shirts, earth shoes, paint-stained pants or ratty hair. I know what you're thinking: that's what people expect you to look like if you're an artist. Sure, if you're at a house party. When someone is going to invest their hard-earned money in you, they want to be assured that you are genuine, responsible and trustworthy.

Try to find a happy medium when choosing your outfit. It's good to have a personal style, as long as it's inoffensive, clean and relatively modest. Remember, you're selling yourself as a professional artist. I can guarantee that the last person a client will trust is someone that looks like they slept in their car and bathed in the local creek. Take ownership and pride in yourself!

MARKETING

WHAT IS MARKETING?

Marketing is the process of business promotion to sell products or services. Marketing, unlike sales, is more about finding out what people want, why they have that need, and how best to present said product or service to satisfy that need. Sales, on the other hand, is the actual act of transacting your product/service from you to your customer.

Defining marketing is a little like water in a sieve. There are hundreds of ways to characterize it. It just depends on whom you ask. I'm willing to bet if you asked 100 people to define marketing you would get 100 different answers. For our purposes, however, I will approach marketing as the setup to the sale. Marketing is seeking out how your work will fit the colloquial "marketplace" and creating a framework with which to present your product to that marketplace.

The great thing about the process of marketing is that it gives you valuable information to complete the sale. Essentially, with good marketing strategy, you have pre-qualified your potential client. By doing that, you eliminate the hard sale from the equation. You want to make selling as simple as possible and by thorough market research specific to your product; you should be able to compile enough information and data to close the sale.

ART MARKETING OR THE ART OF MARKETING

Marketing artwork is no different from marketing any other product. The process remains the same. By doing your homework and making educated decisions, finding potential buyers for your work should be easy. However, unlike marketing cars or beer, your product starts with you. The biggest problem with this is that it is difficult for the artist to switch gear from a creative mindset to a business mindset. It's not always an easy or exciting transition. But, it can be!

As an artist, you're motivated to create your art to satisfy yourself. In the marketing business, the motivation is to satisfy the customer and, ultimately, to make a sale. Two different worlds, right? You may think so. But, the concept for this book was borne with the goal in mind that you will be able to accomplish and perhaps enjoy both. Satisfy your creative needs and, at the same time, be able to meet the needs of a potential buyer.

I have always maintained that the artist should learn basic marketing skills and simple communication skills to be able to identify and relate to someone's needs. Marketing artwork is the ability to identify clients' needs, while simultaneously establishing a relationship and satisfying those needs. It is not for me to say how close to or far away this mindset is from your creative process.

To market yourself and your work, the artist must first be willing to step outside their comfort zone. Artists must challenge themselves to not only create the art but understand and communicate its value to everyone. Sure, you can hire others to sell and represent your work. If money is no issue, then by all means hire an agent or sales rep. However, if you are reading this book then odds are that you want to reap all the benefits of your work. To do this, you will need to invest some time in learning and researching.

The sad truth of most of the artists I know is they do not have the necessary tools, knowledge, desire or confidence to market their work effectively. No one but a select groups of friends and family ever sees (or purchases their work). It might feel like no is out there to help you. But, I believe you're one step ahead of the game by reading this book. I'll help you grab the bull by the horns and learn how to pitch, market and sell your work. So, let's roll up our sleeves and get to work!

MARKETING MANAGEMENT

Marketing management is taking responsibility for the promotion and sales of your work and developing a well thought out plan of action to do so. Included in this plan is: market research and analysis, planning, and implementation. A monetarily successful artist has a savvy marketing brain. Good marketing not only makes the general public aware of you and your work, but creates a desire to acquire. It communicates your product to your consumer.

Marketing and marketing management is an investment in you. It's an investment in your time and, most of all, an investment in your career.

MARKETING ALL AROUND US

Many don't realize that they experience the effects of marketing every day. It is something every business does and something that effects each of our decisions as a consumer on a daily basis— from deciding to go to that chain grocery store instead of the farmer's market or buying one car over another. You practice marketing too, whether you realize it or not. Ever applied for a job? What did you have to do while you sat across from some higher-than-thou HR director? You had to represent yourself accurately and favorably in order to get the job, i.e. sell yourself. This is exactly what marketing is.

Start with an open mind. When artists hear the term 'salesperson', they of a used car dealer, or the suit clad guy going door-to-door with a suitcase full of telephone books— the depressed figure of Willy Loman from Arthur Miller's play, Death of a Salesman. Hollywood usually makes a mockery out of the way salespeople dress and acts. Selling your work doesn't mean you have to become adopt a sleazy, dishonest personality or buy a plaid suit. In fact, marketing artwork effectively is all about being yourself.

THE IMPORTANCE OF OBSERVING

Watch others in your industry and take notes:

- Do they have a certain kind of charm?
- Do they have principles that you can adopt?
- How are they successful? How are they not?
- Are there other people or business that you would want to model?

Let's look at some traits a good salesperson might use in their marketing approach:

- Ask precise questions, because they will give you precise answers.

- Listen, listen, listen to those answers and make notes.
- Be clear and consistent with your message or pitch.
- Always keep in mind what your goals are. For example: My goal is to use my music   demo to book venues for my band. By keeping that goal in mind, you might mention that your music is great live in your marketing literature.
- Constantly be aware of potential problems so your prepare to overcome them
- Be honest with yourself: Who are you? What are your beliefs? Marketing is telling other what you stand for and what core values you will not compromise.
- What will you tolerate and not tolerate?

BIG PHARMA: A GOOD EXAMPLE TO FOLLOW

In my opinion, the best salespeople in the world are working in pharmaceutical sales. However you may feel about the industry, from a marketing standpoint, Big Pharma revolutionized the craft. Not only do they sell their product, they sell hope. Pharmaceuticals is an industry that has efficaciously identified needs, marketed toward those needs and succeeded in building multi-billion dollar global corporations like Johnson & Johnson, Merck & Co., AbbVie, and AstraZeneca. From the frail-boned grandmother on anabolics, to the inner-city schoolteacher who needs to keep her blood pressure controlled, to the growing number of children and teens diagnosed with Attention Deficit Disorder, Big Pharma aggressively markets to each and to their doctors as well.

Big Pharma sales teams have built this staggering prescription drug dependency that the vast majority of Americans consume and kill to get. While this is definitely a hot topic in media coverage and political platforms, my purpose is not to moralize. Big Pharma created HOPE with their magic little pills— hope that suffering would be eased and hope that people would live longer, fuller lives. From a marketing perspective, this is genius.

Pharmaceutical salespeople are the great conversationalists and the great motivators. They make educated people believe in their product and procure massive amounts of celebrity endorsement and funding to get their message across. The reps I have met are funny, usually good looking, drive nice cars, make big money and are hardly ever out of work.

All that said, I know artists probably don't aspire to be like them. However, Big Pharma is a great example of what effective marketing is. They marketed with emotion. They did not just sell their medication, but identified and exploited the allegedly bettering effect of buying and using their medication. You can use this principle in your marketing approach as well. Use emotive marketing and try to be as well dressed, charming, intelligent, and empathetic as you possible can.

There is an old saying: "Salespeople make the world go round." They do, fortunately or not. And the great ones do it effortlessly. Become effortless with your own marketing and sales!

Exercise 1: Prepare Yourself

Here's a little test to find out more about yourself. Grab a piece of paper and be entirely honest.

1. What are my skills? What are my weaknesses? (It doesn't matter if they're business related.)
2. What is my product? Be specific.
3. Who is my target? What are their characteristics?
4. What is my goal? Be concise.
5. How would my work help my customer?
6. Who am I?
7. What do I do?
8. Why am I unique?
9. Why am I better than my competition?
10. What am I passionate about?

Exercise 2: Knowing Your Market = Knowing Your Client

Once you have a potential client in mind, write these questions down and answer them as well as you can. Use your answers to develop a personalized pitch and pare it down to an excellent paragraph.

1. What does your client do for a living?
2. What kinds of wants/needs/desires do you envision this person might have?
3. How can your work satisfy those desires?
4. If your client is a multi-person company, who is the contact person?
5. What is that contact person's role in the company?
6. What kind of company is it?
7. What competitors has your client purchased from before?
8. Why would your work be better for your client than a competitor?
9. What is your market value? I.e. What is your product worth?
10. What kind of compensation is your competition receiving?

PUT IT ON PAPER

Write your pitch down and then re-write it has many times as you can stomach it. Your marketing pitch must exude forethought, intelligence and good sense. Well-prepared pitches should tease the customer and peak their interest. Remember, your marketing materials represent you and are oftentimes the first impression a client would receive. Depending on what you choose to work on first, you can use your pitch to help inform your sales letter or visa versa.

Read what you write and have others proofread your work. Check for:

- Flow. Does each topic flow logically into the next?
- Excitement. Does it make you sound interesting and induce the reader to find out more?
- Grammar & Mechanics. Is spelling, punctuation, sentence structure all correct?
- Impact. Does it make your work sound impressive?

RESUME TIPS

- Be accurate and truthful.

- Use buzzwords in first word of statements. Ex: Implemented new pottery firing technique
- Keep it simple and uncluttered with unrelated information.
- Attach a clean, well-designed business card
- Limit yourself to one page
- Use high-quality paper stock

SOCIAL MEDIA

A recent study done by a few market research firms show that good marketing practices, on average, use 5 social media outlets to expose their business or product. Oftentimes, these social media sites overlap in purpose. However, here is a break-down of what specific sites are usually used for:

Popular Social Networking Sites:

- Facebook
- LinkedIn
- Twitter
- Google+

Popular Photo Sharing Sites:

- Instagram
- Flicker
- Tumblr

Popular Video Channels:

- YouTube
- Vimeo
- Vine

Popular Online Marketplace Communities:

- Pinterest

- Foursquare

- Etsy

FACEBOOK

Facebook is a social networking sensation. The company's advent is immortalized in Hollywood film, The Social Network (2010). Facebook looked at the cadre of MySpace and took it ten steps forward. While it could be said that Facebook has seen a recent decline in membership and use, it still is the most popular hangout spot on the web. Some studies conclude that 80% of web marketers use Facebook. And almost every business out there has a Facebook page. Many producers and executives actually use Facebook "Likes" as a barometer for the popularity and merit of a prospective acquisition.

Facebook is a very useful tool if you consider the exponential reach of a network. Let's break it down: You make a single post about your new sculpture, complete with a nice photo of you with your clay-ridden hands molded over an amorphous shape and another one of the beautiful finished product. Say have you have 200 friends. If half of your friend list shares your post, and each of those friends have 100 friends who share it and those friends have 100 friends who share it… you see where I'm going. By making one post, you've managed to reach thousands. See how beneficial it is? Another thing to keep in mind is to keep posting regularly. Followers of your page might think that you are no longer producing if you don't post about it!

If you decide to use Facebook, be sure to represent yourself professionally. Generate well-written posts and professional comments. Believe me, it's much easier than it sounds. My initial reaction to the negative posts and comments on my page was to become a gunslinger and go after the trolls. It's very difficult to have your work criticized by some putz who thrives on slander and creating drama. Don't get into a pissing contest! It's unprofessional. Remember, you can always block a person or delete a comment.

LINKEDIN

The best way to describe LinkedIn is as a business networking site. Use LinkedIn as a professional marketing tool more than any other social media site. LinkedIn lists and connects professionals in your field. Company pages offer a platform to share diverse types of content. You won't see a lot of brands and corporations on LinkedIn, but rather the people behind such companies. Add a photo and boilerplate information and start sharing. If you work with others, encourage your team to create a profile too and share information about your company. People who work at your organization (especially executives) can connect their personal profiles to your brand, creating a new source of content that your audience can follow. Good connections also lend an air of credibility to your business.

When generating copy for your 'About' sections, think quality, not quantity. Be concise and efficient. LinkedIn users tend to be overwhelmed when certain profiles over-share. Make sure you're only sharing the highest quality content you create for your brand. Bringing in a steady stream of recommendations from clients or partners will provide a renewable source of user-generated content. Leverage those recommendations made by other users because they support the image of a good rapport in your business dealings.

Participating in LinkedIn group discussions is an excellent way to demonstrate professional leadership. Strike up conversations that could lead to new business. Share your content and interact with other group members to establish a strong rapport within the community.

TWITTER

Twitter is rapidly becoming an invaluable marketing tool. It is a site used to relay information in a quick and efficient manner. Try to keep your tweets interesting and consistent.

- Tweet original content.

- Draft well-written text (remember you have a word count limit: 140 characters).

- Use specific information

VIMEO/YOUTUBE

Widespread success of web video content will be around for some time. It seems people would rather watch content than read it. YouTube and Vimeo are two of the biggest platforms to consider. Branding yourself on these channels means you will have to produce a precise message and be able to grab people's attention. A good video editor is a plus, but video-editing software has become more and more accessible to the layman. Remember to be consistent and specific in your videos. Humor is always a great tool on these platforms. Who knows, maybe your video will be the next one to go viral!

GOOGLE+

This platform offers a healthy mix of content media and functions in the same way the Facebook "Like" does— by way of the single-click vote. Google is an all-powerful web presence and it would be smart to figure out how to harness some of that power to promote your business. Google+ gives you the ability to create an eye-catching page experience. Take advantage of it by posting more than just links and text. Mix in a variety of photos, videos, and info-graphics for a healthy-looking page. Share unique content from your staff and highlight personalities with posts from individual staff members to create a friendly and personalized experience.

Hash tags (#) help your posts get discovered through search engines, while the + feature gets the attention of individuals. Google has many tools to help the artist market their work. Experiment with these tools to help your audience find you.

BRANDING

Your brand defines your product and differentiates it from others on the market. Branding is done by developing a cohesive theme and aesthetic for your company. For example, the Coco Chanel brand is elegance and high fashion. Therefore, Coco Chanel would use simple, elegant fonts in marketing material and feature ads with ladies in evening wear. When setting out to define your brand, think about the holistic message you want to get across with your artwork. Are your paintings better suited to a New York penthouse or a Vermont country house? Market and brand accordingly.

What is it that makes you, you?

To define your brand, you must first determine the themes and aesthetic that characterizes your work. Brainstorm adjectives that would fit your work and then make stylistic choices that agree with those words. It's not an exact science, but as an artist, you probably have a better sense of aesthetic than most.

Avoid misleading your market by branding in a way you think fashionable and not accurate to your work. Never brand yourself as something you are not. A great example of this mistake is found in my area where we have a lot of "Award-Winning Filmmakers". In reality, they are amateur video producers at best and the awards they've won are from local film festivals and art shows. By branding themselves as "Award-Winning Filmmakers", they misleads the consumer about what kind of production company they are (Film as opposed to Video) and their success level (Hollywood Foreign Press as opposed to Middletown Film Festival). If you were a bookkeeper, you shouldn't brand yourself as a CPA. Be honest and true to what you do. Someone might call you out one day. If you can't deliver, your reputation is damaged, sometimes irreparably.

Be a player. Have a strong online presence. Be kind and helpful to others. Offer advice. Let people know who you are and what you do.

Network, network, network! Develop a presence by networking online and in-person. Go to industry and community events and connect with others in your field. Sit down for coffee or a beer and talk about your goals. Form relationships with people that do what you do. Always ask for feedback from others. People in your industry know what you're going through. Talk to them about your look, logo and website.

The 3 C's of Branding

1. Clarity
2. Consistency
3. Constancy

Be Very Clear About:

1. Who you are.
2. What you do.
3. Where you want to go.

TIPS FOR ONLINE BRANDING

- You are an expert. Be prepared to answer questions professionally.
- Use your past successes and achievements as a marketing springboard.
- Make it easy for people to contact you with an email you check regularly or contact application on your website.
- Offer free help or advice to others.
- Be kind and cordial to all.
- Communicate well.
- Learn from others in the same business.
- Create and design a professional look and logo. If you don't think you're competent enough to design these things, this is an area where money is well spent to hire a designer.
- Join brand-related communities.
- Share your links and info with others.
- Offer to mentor someone.
- Join internet forums in your field.
- Set up a personal blog with a logo and artwork.
- Invest time in social media such as LinkedIn or Twitter.
- Create a Facebook presence.
- Have a bio page on your website.

- Produce a podcast or video series.

- Setup a YouTube or Vimeo channel.

- Write for other blogs or guest post.

- Write an informal e-book.

- Use emailing to make initial contact, NEVER spam.

- Practice writing using POWER WORDS

- Start a small newsletter.

Once you brand yourself as an expert, be prepared to get into the batter's box. People will call you out on your expertise. By making bold statements, you are necessarily asking others to challenge you. Be prepared to meet that challenge!

MARKETING PLAN

Marketing plans will always differ from business-to-business. However, a well-conceived plan will always have several of the same elements across industry lines. Companies that design a solid marketing plan experience a 20-30% improvement in sales than similar businesses without one. This can be the result of many factors, but being organized and having a focused goal certainly helps any business.

A well-constructed marketing plan answers the following questions:

1. What is your economic and business climate?
2. What are the challenges or problems that you face?
3. What do you hope to achieve?
4. What is your product?
5. Who are your potential customers?
6. Why should people buy your work?
7. How will you reach potential customers?
8. Who are your competitors?
9. How will you measure growth and success?
10. What are the potential objections you will encounter?

MARKET RESEARCH

Market Research is crucial as it pertains to gathering data to inform your plan.

5 ELEMENTS TO CONSIDER

1. MARKET

The answers you generate will give you enough data to evaluate your market. You should constantly do market evaluations as the market is always in a state of flux. Trends change and businesses come and go. It is smart to know where you stand in your marketplace every few months.

- What is your market?
- Who do you need to cater toward?
- What are the trends in your field?
- Is there growth in your field?
- Who and how big are your competitors?
- How fair is your pricing compared with others?
- What kind of marketing/sales does your competition do?
- Does your competition have a weakness?
- Are you up to date with technology?

2. POSITION

Good positioning comes through great market analysis, taking advantage of opportunities and knowing what threatens your business. This is known as SWOT Analysis:

- S>What are your strengths?
- W>What are your weaknesses?
- O>What are your opportunities?
- T>What threatens your organization?

SWOT Analysis sets a good foundation to help you position yourself in the marketplace. It is a strategy that will help you encapsulate your business capabilities.

3. STRATEGY

Every business must have a strategy to move from point A to point B. Your marketing strategy has to center around selling your existing product, finding new markets and buyers, and introducing new products to the market. A clear strategy will help you achieve a logical set of actions to reach your goal. Your strategy will be implemented by taking specific actions or "tactics" that define your plan. What tactics can you deploy? Who will execute them and how long will each tactic be in place to achieve the desired results?

4. INCENTIVES

What can you offer potential customers that others can't? How can you go that extra mile and make your product and service more attractive? Here are some incentive examples:

- Fast shipping
- Smooth transaction
- Free bonus for ordering now
- Guaranteed satisfaction
- Excellent product support
- Competitively priced

5. CALL-TO-ACTION

To illicit the maximum market response, make it simple, quick, and easy to do. The process of purchasing from you should be smooth and hassle-free. You also want quick transaction capabilities to get money in your account!

- One-click purchasing
- Visible phone number and human-to-human contact

- Ordering directly from website
- Easy payments with credit cards and PayPal
- Simple checkout procedure
- Confirmation email that the order went through
- "Thank you" and follow-up emails
- Immediate customer support

MARKETING OBJECTIVES AND STRATEGIES

- Develop and Create Your Marketing Strategy
- Define your brand
- Select a target market
- Establish personal values
- Set funding and fundraising goals
- Analyze your situation and competition
- Monitor and evaluate your plan

CREATE YOUR MARKETING PLAN

By answering the following questions, your marketing plan will began to take form. Try to be as honest and expansive as possible.

- Where am I currently?
- Where do I want to go?
- How can I get there?
- What opportunities am I going to take advantage of?
- Am I willing to invest the time? How much?
- Will this be costly? What is my budget?
- Do I have the resources or do I need backers?

Answer each of these components with honesty. Devote at least a paragraph to each questions.

1. Vision: What is my vision?
2. Mission Statement: What is my mission?

3.   Current Situation: How much time and money do I have to devote?

4.   S.W.O.T (see below)

5.   Objective specific to your work

6.   Your product: Describe your product or your work as accurately as possible.

7.   Projected results: How much income will I generate?

8.   Market analysis: Is there a need in the market right now?

9.   Uniqueness: How can I stand out in the crowd?

S.W.O.T.

- STRENGTHS
- WEAKNESSES
- OPPORTUNITIES
- THREATS

Make a list for each and extrapolate on each listed item:

STRENGTHS:

What are your strengths, in business or life in general?

WEAKNESSES:

Name some areas where you see room for improvement.

OPPORTUNITIES:

What opportunities can you take advantage of? Who do you know that can help you?

THREATS:

What threaten your work? Is your market over-saturated? Are the economic conditions friendly to what you do? Do you suffer from monetary or time constraints?

CAREER STARTUP PLAN

Ask yourself the following questions & answer each in a paragraph accordingly:

- What do you do? What is your vision?
- Identify your target market? Who is it?
- Who can you sell to?
- Assess your competition. Who are they?
- How did your competitors market and advertise their product?
- How do you find new clients?
- What is your absolute goal?
- What objections must you overcome?
- What social resources can you use for product awareness?

SAMPLE

The T.A.S.K Business Plan Worksheet

1. Mission Statement
2. Vision Statement
3. Objectives

        A. Market Analysis

        1) Competition

        2) Selling Groups

        B. Financial Plan

4. Risks

MISSION STATEMENT

Why are you starting a business? What do you hope to accomplish with this business? What makes your work unique and what makes your selling position unique?

VISION STATEMENT

Explain the work you do. Why do you do it?

OBJECTIVES

What do you hope to accomplishing concrete terms:

Business Team: combined skills, experience, biography, applicable abilities

RESOURCES

MARKET ANALYSIS:

(What is the market doing? Is there a need?)

- Who is your market?
- What is the market like?
- Who is your competition?
- Who will purchase your art?
- How competitive is your pricing?

COMPETITION:

- Who are your competitors? How long have they been in business? Who is the top seller?
- What did they do?
- How do they advertise/market?
- Who are their customers?
- What is their product like?
- Compare your skills in the marketplace?

GOALS:

- Projected sales?
- Number of new clients each month?
- Average revenue from each new client?
- In five years, where do you want to be?

YOUR FINANCIAL PLAN:

What is your current revenue status and your sources for grants, funding, loans, etc.

- How much money do you have now?
- How much money do you need to succeed?
- Office space, do you need it?
- Studio space, where will you work?

RISKS:

- How will you pay your bills?
- Do you have insurances?
- Will you hold down a part-time job?
- What happens if you get sick?
- How will you save money?
- Do you have a reinvestment plan?

GOALS WORKSHEET

Create a list of goals and objectives to work toward.

TOP 3 goals for the next:

30 days

1.

2.

3.

60 days

1.

2.

3.

90 days

1.

2.

3.

6 months

1.

2.

3.

CUSTOMER SERVICE

At its most basic level, customer service is an organization's ability to supply their customers' wants and needs. However, this definition leaves out the transactional nature of customer service. For instance, there is a warehouse business model where goods are laid out and customers can choose items themselves and take them to checkout. This model supplies a customer's need for a product or products (assuming the customer finds what he wants), but from the customer's point of view, there's no service involved.

A BETTER DEFINITION OF CUSTOMER SERVICE

Customers assume that customer service involves an interaction with another human being, whether that person helps them find something, choose something or buy something. For businesses, then, another useful definition is that customer service is a business's ability to satisfy its customers.

Companies can have all the elements of customer service in place—from wait-staff to return policies—but if customers are not satisfied with the way their transaction was handled or its results, they won't be back.

The core of good customer service = bringing old customers back and attracting new ones through the "good news" that current customers are spreading about your business.

WHY IS CUSTOMER SERVICE SO IMPORTANT?

Customer service is intrinsic to every successful business. Recent reports state that consistent high performers in customer service are miles ahead of their competition.

The Harvard Business Review reports that if you can prevent 5% of your customers from leaving, you can increase your bottom line profit by 25 – 95%. Many customers leave one business and go to another because of a customer service issue. That said, you have to be very serious about customer service. What is sad is that most of those customers don't bother to complain. They just leave and don't come back. You are then in a situation where you are spending time and money trying to get new customers into your business. With some consistent and persistent training to your team members, or a firm policy for the way in which you deal with customers, you can figure out how to satisfy every customer, every time.

Here are some top tips:

- Listen to complaints - Complaints are a wonderful gift, it is feedback of the highest order. Enjoy them and learn fast.
- Enable your people - Enable and encourage your people to give an immediate and generous customer response
- React fast - Make sure that you and your people work with pace and immediacy with customer issues.
- Be systems focused - Ask, 'What would my customer think of this - would it give brilliant service?' If not, reshape the system fast.
- Be curious - Encourage everyone in your team to overhear, be nosy, and ask questions and feedback information from your customers.
- Research the Marketplace - Do more in your own business from what you experience as a customer elsewhere. Encourage your people to do this as well.
- Have fun with your customers. It builds relationships and relationships are the bedrock of good business.

Customers judge the service level of every business and they're much more likely to share a bad experience with other people than a good one.

According to the White House Office of Consumer Affairs, happy customers who have their issues resolved tell between 4-6 people about their experience. Meanwhile, a dissatisfied customer will tell between 9-15 people about their experience - and about 13% of dissatisfied customers tell more than 20 people about their poor experience.

Data like this is a potential disaster for a small business trying to make their way into the market.

10 CUSTOMER SERVICE TIPS

The "people" aspect of business is what it's all about. Rule #1: Think of customers as individuals, not as a market group. Once we think that way, we realize that good business practice lies in satisfying our customer, not in our product or services. Putting all the focus on the merchandise in our store, or the services our corporation offers, leaves out the most important component: each customer. Keeping those individual customers in mind, here are some easy, down-home customer service tips to keep them coming back!

1. Remember, there is no way that the quality of customer service can exceed the quality of the people who provide it. Think you can get by paying the lowest wage, giving the fewest of benefits, doing the least training for your employees? It will show. Companies don't help customers, people do.

2. Realize that your people will treat your customer the way they are treated. Employees take their cue from management. Do you greet your employees enthusiastically each day? Are you polite in your dealings with them? Do you try to accommodate their requests? Do you listen to them when they speak? Consistent rude customer service is a reflection not as much on the employee as on management.

3. Do you know who your customers are? If a regular customer came into your facility, would you recognize them? Could you call them by name? All of us like to feel important; calling someone by name is a simple way to do it and lets them know you value them as customers. Recently, I signed on with a new fitness center. I had been a member of another one for the past ten years, renewing my membership every six months when the notice arrived. I had been thinking about changing, joining the one nearer my home and with more state-of-the-art equipment. So, when the renewal notice came, I didn't renew. That was eight months ago. Was I contacted by the fitness center and asked why I did not renew? Did anyone telephone me to find out why an established customer was no longer a member or to tell me they missed me? No, and no. My guess is that they didn't even know they lost a long-time customer and apparently, they didn't care.

4. Do your customers know who you are? If they see you, would they recognize you? Could they call you by name? A visible management is an asset. At the Piccadilly Cafeteria chain, the pictures of the manager and the assistant manager are posted on the wall at the food selection line, and it is a policy that the manager's office is placed only a few feet from the cashier's stand at the end of that line, in full view of the customers, and with the door kept open. The manager is easily accessible, and there is no doubt about "who's in charge here." You have only to beckon to get a manager at your table to talk with you.

5. For great customer service, go the extra mile. Include a "Thank-You" note in a customer's package, send a birthday card, clip the article when you see their name or photo in print, write a congratulatory note when they get a promotion. There are all sorts of ways for you to keep in touch with your customers and bring them closer to you.

6. Are your customers greeted when they walk in the door or at least within 30-40 seconds upon entering? Is it possible they could come in, look around, and go out without ever having their presence acknowledged? It is ironic that it took a discount merchant known for price, not service, to teach the retail world the importance of greeting customers at the door. Could it be because Sam Walton knew this simple, but important gesture is a matter of respect, a matter of saying, "We appreciate you coming in." That this has nothing to do with the price of merchandise?

7. Give customers the benefit of the doubt. Proving to him why he's wrong and you're right isn't worth losing a customer. You will never win an argument with a customer, and you should never, ever put a customer in that position.

8. If a customer makes a request for something special, do everything you can to deliver. The fact that a customer cared enough to ask is all you need to know to try to accommodate them. It may deviate from your customer service policy, but (if it isn't illegal) try to do it. Remember that you are making one exception for one customer, not making new policy. Mr. Marshall Field was right-on in his famous statement: "Give the lady what she wants."

9. Do you have customer service associates properly trained in how to handle a customer complaint or an irate person? Give them guidelines for what to say

and do in every conceivable situation. Be sure to make yourself available to handle circumstances that you didn't prepare your associates for. People on the frontline of a situation play the most critical role in your customer's experience. Make sure they know what to do and say to make that customer's experience a positive, pleasant one.

10. Want to know what your customers think of your company? Ask them! Compose a "How are we doing?" card and leave it at the exit or register stand, or include it in their next statement. Keep it short and simple. Ask things like: What do they like? What don't they like? What would they change? What could you do better about their latest experience there? To ensure the customer sends it in, have it pre-stamped. And, if the customer has given their name and address, be sure to acknowledge receipt of the card.

WHAT IS GOOD CUSTOMER SERVICE?

What is good customer service? It's when you make the customer feel good about the decision they made to do business with you. Good customer service is when you sell well, which means you're serving well. For example, if you sell a product that requires batteries, suggest that the customer purchase batteries. This kind of suggestion goes a long way in creating excellent customer service.

Customer service can be defined in a lot of ways, but the key element here is that the customer defines those ways, not you the retailer. We can create formats, but it's up to the customer to accept or reject those formats. So, the next time you go shopping, ask yourself: "Am I getting good or bad customer service. Why or why not?"

SELLING

I just want to make it clear that this book is by no means is trying to convert the artist into a salesperson. The creative process is paramount. Even if you have little-to-no sales training you can still learn the basic principles needed to be able to pitch and sell your work.

I learned many years ago that there is NO ONE that is going to take your work more seriously than YOU! I like to refer artists to a helpful phrase: "You own it!". This means that you have to see it through, take pride in what you do, and be responsible for its failure or success. I find just by saying, "I own it", I become very protective as well as proud of what I have done. It also becomes a motivating tool to sell your work. "You own it", now go and find someone to buy it.

Having someone else sell your art is fine as long as they have the desire to do so. That desire for someone not attached to the work is money. How much can they make selling your work? Putting all of your faith in someone that has no emotional attachment to the work is what people do every-day. The attitude for someone that has no emotional attachment to a product is: I'll invest my energy in a product that I can sell. If not, I have other products that will sell.

This section should be easily comprehensible and lend some helpful skills for your selling process. I was told many times in my career that people just don't share the same passion you do about your work. It is a job for them; they get a commission and that's where their commitment ends. I hope that some of these tips and techniques will help you turn your passion into sales!

I would like to share with you a few real life' experiences that illustrate the effectiveness of the following theories. When I decided to cultivate my sales skills in the early 80s, there was one person revered as the salesperson guru: Zig Ziglar. I read all of his books, took notes, and absorbed whatever he had to say. I digested that information, customized it to my particular field, and tailored it to what I wanted to do and where I wanted to be.

During the writing of this book, I kept telling myself, I need to test my theories and techniques so I can document them. I am a straightforward guy. I want to give out useful information. Information that works. After all my name is on this book; I want it to represent what I truly believe. Thus, I had to apply my theories in the real life situations. My past successes were great, but could I take my notes and make it work right now?

I decided to talk with some artist friends of mine who lacked the skills that I have had the fortune to acquire. They were green to the business side of filmmaking, so I took on a couple motion picture projects with the goal of securing a few distribution deals for each filmmaker by using the very same technique and principles that I will alter outline. Sure, I could talk the talk, but could I walk the walk?

So, I was about to apply what I had learned and practiced for other artists, projects in which I had no stake. The results were far beyond my expectations:

I decided to start with my friends, Bill and Tiff McLean, who are local filmmakers that helped me many times on my film projects. The McLeans just finished their film: How to Kill a Zombie. We sat down to talk about their goals and how I could help them. The goal was defined: Get the film sold! Therefore, the next few days after our meeting, I went through my industry contacts (this can be done just as easily through industry research) and found the perfect fit for this film. The company was Maxim Media International, the largest independent horror distributor in the world. I began with a nice email and followed up with a persuasive phone conversation explaining that if they put this film in their catalog, it would be a win-win situation for us both. The process was lengthy. It took a few weeks before they could see the film. Yet, by this time, I had prompted them to want to see the film. A couple of days after screening the film, they emailed me to say it was everything I said it was and that this could very well be a money maker! I followed up with another phone call to discuss this with them. Maybe it was because I did not have the pressure of this being my film or maybe it was because I had the confidence of success in selling my own films, but either way, my pitch went very smoothly. I knew I had nailed the sale. We had How to kill a Zombie signed to a worldwide motion picture deal in 75 countries. This was certainly a feather in my cap and it also reinforced my notes. However, I did not stop there. Could I do it again? This time with someone I didn't know and whose films I had never watched?

Another filmmaker I only knew from Linked In contacted me about his film. He had heard that I helped Bill & Tiff sign a distribution deal, could I help him? He had a dramatic film. I would have to change gears. Zombies were a hot topic according to many distributors, but how about a drama? To see if his drama film could sell, I knew my preparation had to be much different—different genre, different distributors. The rub here was that I did not know this filmmaker. We talked on the phone and agreed that I would give it a shot.

I applied the same structure and put together a sales and artist plan and then began to contact distributors, many distributors I never met or talked to before. I drafted a classic, well thought out email to grab their attention. I sent over the links to his movies. The filmmaker had asked if the distributers would screen his three films. This was unusual, so I made another phone call and they agreed to screen all of them with no guarantees. I sent the three online links to the films in my next email. They confirmed they had received them. And then we waited.

I made a few follow up calls just to remind them of the projects. It was only a little over a week later that we heard back from them. The offer came in for another worldwide distribution deal. It was a state-of-the-art digital distribution deal to all the major online/V.O.D/cable and satellite outlets as well as online retail outlets. The deal was huge in exposure, not just for one film for but for all three! The filmmaker was ecstatic! I was able to sell not only one of his films but I secured a three-movie deal using the same principles that I have been writing in this book. Bolstered by this, I decided to try it a third time.

I was then challenged with helping a musician friend of mine. This time I was aiming to get the musician signed to a management deal from the UK. I plugged in different verbiage but used the same tactics and it worked there as well. Confidence came once my musician client signed his deal overseas. The management and recording deal is in the UK and I will be going over there sometime soon to have a pint! The point here is that you can do this too! The same sales principals will work regardless of the art medium.

I can now provide my own testimonial: I have real world experience and results to exhibit in this book. People are people. Making a sale is entrusted by mutual respect and genuine enthusiasm. If you truly believe, it will show. Being professional, speaking clearly, being confident and being prepared is all you need to do.

SELLING YOURSELF AND SELLING YOUR WORK

1.   UNDERSTANDING THE SALES GAME:

Understanding the selling game means being prepared and accepting that you are the best person available to sell your work. Creating a solid sales environment means that you will need to work hard on techniques that will help you get your product into the public eye. The goal here is to accomplish the following:

- Make yourself look good on paper.
- Prepare yourself to make a sale.
- Practice strategic networking.
- Look like a professional.
- Keep in mind your ABC's: Always Be Closing.

Taking the sale process serious is a difficult challenge for any artist. It means switching your brain from the creative thought to the business thought. You have to have the ability to put your game face on, change any stereotypes you may have about salespeople, and keep an open mind.

No one will buy from you if you don't value yourself first!

Recognize past achievements and be proud of your accomplishments. Highlight achievements and events that have gotten you to this point. To do this you will need the following:

- Passion and belief in what you do.

- Pride! i.e. feel what you say.

- The ability to handle rejection.

- Positive attitude.

- The knowledge that others with less confidence have been successful in selling themselves.

A professional countenance: selling yourself does not mean acting like a used car salesman. Don't be rude, selfish or overly aggressive.

The mindset to ask questions, but most importantly, to listen.

Humility.

A strong set of principles: sell yourself, not who you think you are.

2. PITCHING YOURSELF

There is an old saying which retains its truth today:

Failing to prepare is preparing to fail.

Prepare yourself to pitch yourself and your work. Like a great musician or athlete, preparation comes with practice. The more information you have, the better prepared you will be. If you go into the sales phase half-assed you will be truly disappointed. My hope is that readers of this book are willing to commit to selling their work. If you don't have that commitment, or are not willing to take the sales process seriously, then perhaps you need to reassess your confidence level and commitment. I strongly urge you to do so!

SALES TIPS

- Develop a personal marketing plan (see "Marketing" section).
- Be honest with yourself.
- Know your key strengths.

- List your achievements.

- Know your expertise.

- Why you? Be prepared to answer that.

- Be absolutely clear as to what you want to achieve.

- Know your target market.

- Know what your goal is exactly.

- Know how your work can help your customers.

- Find out your customers' needs.

- Don't be afraid to ask for what you want.

- Know your value among your competition.

- Research your market and your industry.

- Constantly pitch yourself— this is how you network effectively.

- Never wait for people to come to you.

- Know what your potential clients are looking for.

- Always ask what they need if you are not sure.

3. LOOKING GOOD ON PAPER

Looking good on paper is developing an impressive resume or C.V. While it is okay to embellish within reason, a resume full of lies will certainly catch up to you. Some tips to making yourself look good on paper:

- Use the written word to entice and stimulate reader.

- Use powerful verbiage (refer to section on "Power Words").

- Keep writing simple and to the point.

- Use words to make yourself interesting.

- Always highlight the good.

- List only the relevant experience.

- Keep your writing dynamic.

- Be truthful, clear and precise.

4.   GOING IN FOR THE SALE

Remember to prepare before entering into a sales situation. A few things to remember:

- You are the product first and foremost.
- Always make direct contact with decision makers.
- Be polite, cordial and relaxed.
- Use your network and friends to get in touch with potential clients.
- Focus on what you have to offer them right now.
- Use social media to bolster your pitch.
- Have a consistent, thought-out sales mission.
- Sell yourself each and every day, in-person and online.
- Join discussion forums and groups; some can be very helpful in terms of networking or information.
- Strive to make new contacts on LinkedIn, Facebook or Twitter.
- Maintain high-energy, always have that smile in your voice.

5.   NETWORKING YOURSELF

- Join groups of like-minded people.
- Keep an email database.
- Offer to help others, even for free.
- Always have a clean, concise focus plan ready.
- Attend networking events specific to your field.

6.   LOOKING THE PART

Looking like a beatnik may be cool in some parts of the city, but when meeting with restaurant owners that want to put original artwork in their restaurants, it won't fly. Take ownership of your appearance. If you want them to spend money on you, look like you've spent money on yourself.

- Dress to fit into your group.
- You will be selling to people that are professional.

- Maintain good hygiene.
- Body language is important.
- Be alive and sharp.
- Be humble, there are thousands just like you and your customer can buy from them just as well.
- Avoid torn or ripped clothes.
- Brush your hair and/or shave.

10 SALES PRINCIPLES

1. **ATTENTION:** The best salespeople capture the attention of their prospects. They can stand out in a crowd and influence someone that may be otherwise distracted.

2. **LIKABILITY:** People buy from people they like. People interact best with people that they like. Therefore, be likable, interesting, caring, and kind.

3. **LIEF:** Use your personality to influence people to believe that things can and will get better by working with you. But, YOU have to believe first!

4. **TRUST:** Trust works hand-in-hand with belief. People put their trust in you to help them. Once they trust you, they will believe in you. Trust is the foundation of the sale.

5. **EMOTIONAL BOND:** People never remember the words you say, but they always remember the feeling. Whether it is a story or making them laugh, touching the emotions will always get a response. Telling stories and having them relate is one way to secure an emotional bond.

6. **DESIRE:** Desire is looking forward from where you are to where you want to be. The more you can stoke someone's desire and change his or her reality, the easier it will be to influence him or her.

7. **JUSTIFICATION:** People buy with their hearts and justify it in their minds. You need to prove that a product has worked successfully in the past. Use testimonials.

8. **INDIFFERENCE:** A great salesperson has an emotional detachment from the sale. "If you buy from me great! If not, that's great too!" Prospective buyers can feel when a seller is desperate. Play it cool.

9. **OWNERSHIP:** You cannot influence someone unless they own the decision process. Also, you can't get the janitor to make the decision to purchase 100 units; you must pitch to the person that owns the power (pun intended).

10. **INVOLVEMENT:** Having first-hand involvement will always bring more passion to the sale. Buying is the same way. Get your potential client involved in the process, be it via advertising or marketing. Making them invest time and become involved will certainly influence their decision.

SIMPLE STEPS FOR SUCCESS

- Believe in yourself and your product 100%
- Positive attitude and enthusiasm
- Positive talk
- Optimistic outlook
- Believe that you have the best product

Grab Attention

- Packaging is sleek and/or creative
- Work looks professional
- Your dress and hygiene are appropriate
- Smile
- Put on a pleasant and 'accessible' expression

Name Dropping

- Use names of previous customers
- Make sure the clients knows your name and company name

Observing the Other Person

- What is their body language saying?
- Are they comfortable with you?
- Are they listening to you? Are they distracted?
- Not listening means they are not interested; call that to their attention.
- Prepare for the first few minutes or your meeting will be awkward.
- Listen, and Look Like You're Listening!
- Eye contact, head nodding, leaning in to hear
- Facial expressions, smiles and reactions to what they say
- Occasional questioning

You Are Interested

- You can be interesting, if you are interested
- Value the other person's opinions and their time
- Give well-placed compliments
- Have a genuine knowledge of their business
- Mirroring Behavior
- Speak at the same pace
- Use similar gestures
- Use the same keywords that they use frequently
- Speak at the same volume they do

Talking Positively

- Use positive comments in your sentence
- A rainy day sucks.—> It's good for the garden!
- Spin a negative into something good throughout conversation
- Warm and Friendly
- Stay calm
- Don't look or sound stressed
- Pleasant voice and speech
- Non aggressive, fast or intimidating movements

SELLING YOUR PRODUCT BY SELLING YOURSELF

BASIC PRINCIPLES:

- Know your product inside and out
- Believe in yourself: You are the best at what you do.
- Know how your product can enhance their life.
- Remember the 3 I's:
- Intelligence
- Integrity
- Initiative

COMMUNICATION SKILLS:

- Selling yourself is no different from selling a product or an idea.
- The client has to believe in you first.
- Be positive, warm, open and alert.
- Don't talk only about yourself or make false promises.
- Learn to accept rejection: you can't and won't win them all.
- Don't waste people's time. Know your facts and rehearse your pitch.
- Love what you do and let that show!
- Use mirroring techniques to copy their body language and words they use.

THE ART OF NEGOTIATION

A negotiation is the mutual discussion and arrangement of terms to arrive at an agreement or transaction. In any negotiation, the following elements are important and likely to affect the ultimate outcome of a sale:

- Attitude
- Knowledge
- Interpersonal Skills

WHEN DO WE NEGOTIATE?

Every day in your daily activities

Negotiation takes place at the store, in the office, in your studio, etc….

You negotiate with yourself whenever you purchase something: Is the cost right? Can I afford this? We constantly negotiate with ourselves to decide if we are getting a deal. Apply this mindset when negotiating with your customer.

We negotiate dates, vacations, and meetings. It's a constant process.

Some people are very good and negotiating, some are not. That's how it is.

The ULTIMATE GOAL of any negotiation is to come out with a win/win result. Obviously, this won't happen every time, but that should be your mindset when going in.

THINGS TO DO AND NOT TO DO WHEN NEGOTIATING

BAD TACTICS:

There are good and bad tactics in any negotiation. You should avoid the following habits as they can be deal breakers:

- Arguing with your client
- Losing your temper
- Lying
- Cheating your client
- Pointing fingers at the competition
- Bad mouthing others
- Making your client feel sorry for you
- Using negative language and/or swearing
- Insulting anyone
- Being rude or having an attitude > NO DIVAS!

GOOD TACTICS:

Here are some things you should practice in each and every negotiation:

- Logical thinking and reason
- Analysis of the company and buying situation
- Fairness
- Common sense
- Keep in mind that a successful negotiation has two winners: "A line as two sides"
- Inspire a good feeling on both side about what transpired
- Offer free advice or help
- Follow up— Helping with a problem necessitates a follow-up.

OVERCOMING AN IMPASSE:

In every negotiation, there will be a time when everything seems to come to a standstill. Sometimes negotiations break down. We have all been witness to this. Even our own government reaches a gridlock at times. We have seen sporting teams go on strike, whole corporations getting shut down, teachers on strike, and even entire police and fire departments walk out on the job. A negotiation is not a sure thing. It can turn out bad. For our purposes, we are talking about a small negotiation between a few people. It induces far less stress than having our government come to a complete halt. Yet, in either case, a negotiation does follow a protocol. It is a give-and-take discussion. Some things to think about before you get into a negotiation:

- Don't stress out.
- Wear a poker face (you want them to think you don't care).
- NEVER give away a secret that can be used against you.
- Take a break if you have hit a brick wall.
- Control your temper.

- If it's really bad and you are getting no-where, reschedule for a time when you both have time to clear your heads.

A FUNNY NEGOTIATION ANECDOTE

Many years ago, I was in a negotiation with a band that was about to be signed by CBS records. I had directed their music video in Newport, Rhode Island. We had all the terms for payment laid out— it was broken into thirds: ⅓ at pre-production, ⅓ after production and ⅓ Cash On Delivery (C.O.D.). Being that I was a director, my negotiating skills were limited. However, with my experience in the business, I knew how to get the upper hand.

The music video was completed and payment of the last third was due. We agreed to meet with the band while they were on their way to New York to meet with CBS Records. They had their meeting schedule to the minute. They gave me a beer and revealed their hand at the very beginning of the meeting. At that point, no matter what they wanted to pull, I had them "dead in the water", so to speak. Their lawyer was meeting them at CBS at their scheduled time

The meeting started out fun. We joked and talked about the shoot when the leader of the band decided to be brave and said: "We don't think we should have to pay you the full final third as we picked up all the expense." The final payment was for $8,000 if I remember correctly. There was dead silence between my team and the band. So, what was going through my mind?

Well, I knew they needed to leave and catch their flight to meet the record company. I knew that they owed me eight grand. I knew that the record company wanted to see the video before they would sign them. I knew that they were paying a New York lawyer $300 an hour to meet there on time. I also knew that they were playing a dangerous game because my assistant director was sitting with the master video on her laptop. All they knew was that they didn't want to pay the final installment. They had seen a rough cut of the video that was watermarked and therefore useless to implement. What was my move?

I called the waitress over and ordered a huge piece of carrot cake and more coffee. Yes, carrot cake! I was going to make them sweat. They couldn't leave without the master video and it was getting close to their departure time to get to the airport. I had my team get more coffee and we sat and drank. They asked what deal could we make. I slowed everything down: my conversation, the eating of my cake, the drinking of my coffee. Finally, I said: Nothing. There's nothing we can do. You owe me $8,000 or you don't get the master and you spent all that money for nothing. They apparently thought that with their lawyer and CBS waiting, that I would say, "Sure! No problem. Give me half."

They showed their hand too early. All I had to do was detain them from their flight, which would have made them late to NYC, blown the deal, and ring up lawyer costs. I said, "It's getting close to your flight. Cut me a check and let's go." I thought it was done deal. They, however, proceeded to explain how much it cost to put my people up, the models, the limos, and that they didn't need or want all that stuff in the first place. Their lawyer had instructed them to get us to back down or he will take action. This struck me as funny: Our contract had noted all the set terms and they couldn't sue us if they wanted to. As crazy as it seems, they pleaded their case and quickly, mind you.

I wasn't budging. In fact, I had more coffee and let them talk on. They were actually supposed to have left for the airport but now were running late. One of the other band members finally spoke up and said, "Cut them a check. We have to go." Their entire plot was planned to get me to let them slide. I didn't. They cut the check. I made them pay for lunch and while they were on the way to the airport, I cashed the check.

Funny how it turned out: They missed the flight and got to New York late. Their lawyer had left the record company and the CBS record deal fell through. While this was horrible for my client, my team got paid. The point to the story is to dig for information and not to show your hand too soon. If you can get that little nugget that gives you leverage, USE IT. Hopefully, your clients won't be as stupid as these guys were.

THE GOLDEN RULES OF NEGOTIATION

- Listen and listen carefully
- Keep issues relevant and focused
- Avoid giving away too much information about your own position
- Talk about what you can do
- Observe the other person
- Mirror their behavior and speech
- Be courteous and timely
- Using humor to relax them
- Think outside the box
- Emphasize your sacrifice and minimize theirs
- Be comfortable with silence
- Convince them that you have many options to help them
- Cooperation, not conflict
- Reveal no fear or concern
- Never tip your hand

ASK THE IMPORTANT QUESTIONS

- What "wants" do we have in common?
- How can we both get what we want?
- What can we compromise on?

ADDITIONAL TIPS

- Be prepared: Know your client or buyer
- Relax and break the ice with humor if you can
- Speak clearly and practice good communication techniques
- Make the extra effort to actually care and listen
- Be yourself and speak naturally
- Be inviting, not standoffish
- Smile and make people feel comfortable

- Use simple gestures
- Choose action words that exude friendliness
- Stay calm, implement positive thinking
- Speak with pride in your work

IMPORTANT TECHNIQUES

Be Honest: If you don't know, don't guess. Be proactive, however, and pledge to find out.

- Pose the question again should you get confused.
- Keep eye contact and talk to them as you would a friend without being too overly familiar.
- Stay focused on your pitch and what you know
- Know that you are the expert. This is your work.

Confidence Comes With Being Totally Prepared: Rehearse potential objections be prepared with avenues to overcome.

- Practice your pitch and presentation like an actor would with a script.
- Have your pitch organized.
- Prepare your words by using words that sell (see section on "Words").
- Use simple language.
- Be dynamic and show personality.
- Edit your presentation before you go into a meeting.
- Communicate ideas that may help them and offer free advice.
- Offer ideas that may be potential solutions to their problems.
- Be likable and funny.

10 TIPS TO OVERCOME OBJECTIONS

Some people insist that the true test of a salesperson is their ability to overcome objections. Many people welcome the challenge of an objection while others dread them. The best way to overcome an objection is by being prepared. Objections occur when there is lingering doubt or unanswered questions in the mind of the prospect. The prospect may be favorably inclined to make a purchase but might need clarification, more concessions, or approval by another party.

It is almost guaranteed you will get objections if you've failed to establish need, rapport, credibility, or trust. Have you qualified the buyer and determined need and interest level? Here are ten strategies for identifying the true objection and then conquering it:

1. **ESTABLISH MUTUAL TRUST AND CONFIDENCE:** Let the prospect know that you are there to be both an advocate and a consultant. If you can establish a rapport to build a friendship, that is certainly valuable, but not essential.

2. **LISTEN CAREFULLY TO THE OBJECTION BEING RAISED:** Is it an objection or just a delaying tactic? A prospect often will repeat an objection if it is real. To uncover the truth, try asking:

   "Do you really mean . . ."

   "So, you are telling me . . . However, I think you mean something else."

3. **QUALIFY IT AS THE ONLY TRUE OBJECTION:** Ask the prospect if it is the only reason he/she won't buy from your company.

4. **CONFIRM IT AGAIN:** Rephrase your question to ask the same thing twice. Example: Ask, "In other words, if it weren't for the price, you'd buy my service. Is that true?"

5. **PHRASE A QUESTION IN A WAY THAT INCORPORATES THE SOLUTION:** "So, if I were able to get you a longer warranty, would that be enough for you to make a decision?"

6. **ANSWER THE OBJECTION IN A MANNER THAT THOROUGHLY RESOLVES THE ISSUE.** Pull out your guerrilla tactics here. You can submit a testimonial letter, a competitive comparison chart, or a special time-sensitive or price-related offer.

7. **THIS IS THE TIME TO DEMONSTRATE VALUE, LIST COMPARISONS, AND PROVE BENEFITS:** If you cannot answer the

prospect in a way that is different or sets you apart from others, you'll never close this (or any) sale.

8. **ASK A CLOSING QUESTION OR COMMUNICATE IN A HYPOTHETICAL WAY:** Ask a question, the answer to which confirms the sale. Ex: "If I could do X, Y or Z, would you give me your order?

9. **DESCRIBE SIMILAR SITUATIONS WHEN YOU CLOSE:** people like to know about others in the same situation.

10. **CONFIRM THE ANSWER AND THE SALE (IN WRITING WHEN POSSIBLE):** Get the prospect to transform into a customer with a confirming question like:

"When would you like it delivered?"

"When is the best day to begin?"

Product knowledge, creativity, sales tools, and confidence in yourself, your product, and your company must achieve a kind of synergy if you are to overcome sales objections and close the sale. You must combine technique with honesty and conviction to get the prospect to resolve any lingering doubt or conflict.

OVERCOMING PRICE OBJECTIONS

There are many tactics you can employ to overcome cost objections, but you first need to understand their motivations. Most fall into three categories:

1. An "over budget" objection is about money. You need to understand whether the budget can be altered.

2. A "seems pricey" objection is about both money and value. You need to convince the prospect that you will give them value for their money.

3. Others just like to haggle regardless of their situation. Anticipate hagglers by being alert for clients who ask for the best price from the start or micro-managers who are often as concerned about pennies as they are about commas. Quote high- hagglers will be happy with any "deal" they negotiate. Usually, you can get the price you would have offered in the first place.

Once you know the type of objection you are facing, you can decide whether to hold fast on the price you quoted or work with the client to get your wage where they want it.

TRICKS TO GET YOUR QUOTED RATE

The key here is to help the client see why you are worth the price. Here are some tactics:

- Sell the client on a quick turnaround. You can complete the job before they even find another artist.

- Itemize costs they save with you, such as your knowledge, which saves them paying for research time.

- Paying bottom dollar has embarrassed many companies. Remind the client of this.

- Stress how good you are and how effective your results will be. If you don't demonstrate value, the client might look for someone more willing to haggle.

- Compare your fees to the competition's pricing, unless you command top dollar. Position yourself as "reasonable" to overcome cost objections.

- Offer something extra as a free bonus for signing quickly.

Tips to lower your price without selling out!

If it is clear that you DO need to lower the price, but you don't like slave wages, here are some tactics to try:

- Identify steps the client can take to reduce your workload so you can lower your price to their desired level. Sometimes this makes the client realize that it is worth paying you full price after all.

- Offer a cash-back incentive for speedy feedback or proper input from the client. Client cooperation can reduce your workload, so it might be worth lowering your price.

- Look to outsource parts of the project to students. Research? Editing? Can you lower your price this way without working for less?

- Offer a payment plan — three installments work well. This is of no importance for large clients, but smaller clients love it.

- Suggest scaling down the project. If they really have funds for part of it, offer to do just that part of it. This also can make the client decide to pay full price for the entire project.

- Divide a project into phases. Determine what you can do within their budget, and call it Phase I. Chances are they will pay full price for Phase II later on.

- If you remain at a stalemate on price, it is time to decide how badly you want this job. Just remember that when you accept a lower price, you are raising expectations for the next time and lowering your value forever.

CONFIDENCE

Public speaking is a common fear and it can be highly anxiety-inducing. This fear is characterized by a lack of confidence. You might fear that you will be received poorly. However, confidence is a skill that can be learned. Lacking confidence can lead to any of the following: Stress, tension, self-consciousness, speech difficulties, sweating, disorganized thoughts, rapid pulse, dry mouth, and/or discomfort.

You can learn to be confident!

A lack of confidence can be sensed by your client. You might be perceived as lacking competence and this might deter them from doing business with you. The greater your confidence, the stronger your impact will have. Remember, this is confidence, not to be mistaken for cockiness.

RELAXING TECHNIQUES TO HELP INSTILL CONFIDENCE

Breathe slowly to control your body and relax your mind: Breath is the seed of relaxation. Slow, even breaths will focus your mind and reset any outward signs of anxiety. It will also help you formulate your thoughts and contribute to an even, assured speech pattern. Never gasp for breath during speeches; this shows a lack of confidence and disorganized thought processes. Maintain control of your body and mind by controlling your breathing, speaking clearly and pacing yourself.

Pause and reset yourself: Ask for a break if you feel overly anxious. Stop, stand up straight, close your eyes, and take two or three concentrated breaths from your diaphragm. This will put you in a relaxed state. Be sure you are ready, then regroup and return to the meeting.

PSYCHOLOGICAL SELLING

It has been purported that psychological studies can trace specific behavior of human beings in hopes of predicting future behavior. While statistical generalizations can be made, I believe that there is no easy way to predict what people will or will not do in a given situation. People surprise you constantly. However, there are some basic rules that marketing specialists apply to the psychology of marketing and selling. While some work, I believe it is how your client perceives you during that first impression. Nevertheless, here are some important things to consider in psychological selling:

1. **EMOTIONAL DECISION MAKING:** People make decisions based on intuition, desire, or feeling, and usually not on reason or logic. Emotional persuasion is paramount in your written materials.

2. **FACTS ARE HOW PEOPLE JUSTIFY EMOTIONAL DECISIONS:** When buying a car, people don't make a purchase based on the color or how they feel when driving it. They need to be presented with the facts: warranty, gas mileage, safety features, insurance, etc.…

3. **EGO PLAYS A COLOSSAL ROLE:** People are essentially egocentric, meaning that everything they do revolves around themselves and how they feel. Your writing and sales pitch must shed light on the unspoken question: What's in it for me?

4. **EVERYONE WANTS A DEAL!:** People want to feel assured that they got value in any given deal. You must demonstrate that there is a greater value here than the price. You ensure this by instilling value in your work. Example: My work is unique. My work is one-of-a-kind.

5. **PEOPLE ARE SOCIAL ANIMALS:** People are also creatures of habit. In order to survive, we are always willing to interact with others. We might do this to show that we can hold an intelligent conversation or that we are experts in our field. Whatever the reason, your written materials need to include things like people's names, personal anecdotes, pictures, quotes, and/or testimonials.

6. **PEOPLE DO WHAT THEY WANT:** In terms of sales, this means that all you can do is present the facts, give them a good deal and tell them how their life will benefit from your product. If your product can meet their needs, than it is more likely they will purchase from you.

7. **PEOPLE LOVE TO SHOP:** People love to be sold on new products or gadgets. Anything that has the remote possibility of enhancing their life they will buy. The theory here is that selling to people is not as effective as helping them improve their life. A good product with an attractive deal will always sell.

8. **CURIOSITY:** Remember the idiom: "There's a sucker born every minute"? This is not generally the case. Most people are moderately skeptical. They don't like to be cheated or tricked into buying something. Back up all claims by using the testimonials of satisfied customers.

9. **WE ARE ALWAYS SEARCHING:** People are constantly searching for something, be it love, money, glory, success, happiness, or acceptance. It's a never-ending life task. Your goal in selling should be to help your customer identify a need and then fill that need with your work.

10. **PEOPLE ARE NATURALLY LAZY:** Make it easy and it will sell itself. If people could find everything they needed at the corner store, that's where they would always be. People love the convenience of buying when it's easy for them to do so. Make it convenient for them to buy from you.

11. **MOST PEOPLE LIKE THE "HANDS-ON" APPROACH:** There are some people that will never buy online. This is quickly changing, however. The majority of people like to kick the tires and feel like they are in control of their decision. Examine how people shop and remember that the sensory experience is a very big part of how people buy.

12. **THE MAJORITY OF PEOPLE ARE FOLLOWERS, NOT LEADERS:** Look no further than Black Friday to justify this statement. People need to be part of the "in-crowd". They look for deals that others are getting so they won't be outdone. Creating and/or marking a hip product will always guarantee you sales with those that want to be up on the latest.

These are just a few ways that marketers use to tap into the psychology of selling. Use them to design your written materials and the way in which pitch a sale. The most important things to remember is to think about how you would approach buying something and translate those terms to your potential customer. Figure out what motivates them.

A.B.C.

ALWAYS BE CLOSING

Some people are always selling themselves. They pitch themselves in a relaxed manner and fold it seamlessly into normal conversation. Many times it's part of their personality. To these individuals, selling and closing the deal are second nature. It does come naturally to some and others have to work harder to pitch naturally.

For others, a phone conversation might even give them an anxiety attack. As an artist who wants to pitch their own product, you will need to find some sort of middle ground. To get over many of these phobias, all it really takes is practice:

If you fear or hate talking on the phone, start by making more phone calls with friends or people you know won't judge you.

If you don't like speaking to strangers, practice by saying hello to some in public spaces like groceries or train stations where there is no real consequence.

If you really hate large crowds, integrate yourself into groups in a graduation way. You might begin with fun events like fairs or carnivals, where there is a happy environment. Then you can move on to conferences and seminars.

There is no real reason to feel uncomfortable around people. People are people; they are no better or worse than you. Chances are, they too are afraid of being judged and share many of the same anxieties that you do. One technique that I operate under is trying not to be impressed or intimidated by anyone in my field. As a filmmaker, many people ask who my favorite director is. "I don't have one," I say. Usually, I go on to say that given the same cultural and social situation and the same opportunities (such as the nepotism of Hollywood, i.e. Coppolas, Sheens and Sutherlands), I could be as good if not better. Our idols are just people, same as you or I. You are just as talented, but by lacking the opportunities that others may have had, you need to work harder!

You can be excellent!

Excellent in your preparation,

Excellent in your written materials, and

Excellent in your look and speech.

All this said, sometimes you aren't able to close a deal. You may walk away feeling that you have wasted everyone's time, especially yours. You might feel completely discourage when things don't go your way. Success does not occur in quitting. To be successful: NEVER QUIT. Colonel Sanders of KFC was famously rejected 1009 times before he could find a buyer for his now world-wide franchise. If a man in a bolo tie can face rejection and overcome, so can you!

Some Simple Reminders:

- Don't rest! Dropping the ball at the final stages of a sale means certain disaster.
- The entire concept behind marketing is to get the sale. Keep this ultimate goal in mind.
- Perpetuate focus and consistency in your message.
- Stay relaxed and confident.
- Never, never show up late to a meeting. Many artists and musicians I know are never on time. When dealing with other artists you can get away with this. When dealing with business people, distributors or executives, lateness is a deal breaker. Show respect for yourself and a respect for them and their time. Be early if you can.
- Be very specific. At this stage you better know: 1.)What you are selling. 2.)What your customer needs.

- Ask! If there is ever a doubt about what your prospective client needs, take the straightforward approach and ask. Ask for the contract, ask for the job and be prepared to follow up with your pitch.

THE ACTUAL SALE

Don't let the word "sale" intimidate you. We sell ourselves every day. You don't even realize how much you actually market and sell on a daily basis. No matter what you do when dealing with people, you are attempting to make an idea, a concept, product, or even yourself attractive. This is the principle behind selling.

Most of my marketing and selling techniques and tips have been discussed at length. When closing a deal, be sure to keep them in mind. Remember to take notes during previous discussions with your client. These can come in handy if there are any questions or concerns that crop up during the final stages. Get every term discussed in writing if you can, especially if the sale is for a commission of work that you haven't already generated. You want to be flexible with your client, but you have to make sure that you don't get the short end of the deal.

Last, but not least, relax! You've done it! Remember to act with humility and thank your client for their business. Making the sale easy and pleasurable is a great way induce repeat business.

SEALING THE DEAL

- BE strong
- BE consistent
- Be prepared to handle all questions. They may not all be easy.
- Be organized: use notes, charts, and testimonials.
- Never be late to a meeting.
- Put on a confident front, even if you are nervous.
- Prepare your short, concise pitch.
- Offer ways your art will help them with their problems.
- Avoid bumbling and filler speech, ie. "Um" "Uh".

- Acknowledge the other person by using "you" to reinforce what they said.

- Ask what the next step is and how you can work together.

- Send a follow-up email or phone call a few days later.

- Be yourself.

- You won't sell everyone, that's just life.

NETWORKING

Expose yourself! No, not in that way. I'm talking about the kind of exposure you get for your work by networking and advertising. Exposure is a necessity to find people that will potentially buy your work or people who can connect you to others who will. Network through artist groups and websites like Meet Up, Craigslist or LinkedIn. LinkedIn is my personal favorite for viable business connections. As was described, LinkedIn connects your business with other professionals and professional clientele. Unlike Facebook, Linked-In users are not prone to announce what they had for dinner.

Ask around and talk to people you know. Let others know what you are doing and be prepared to speak intelligently about what you do. You may even offer friends a finder's fee if they help you hook up with a new client. If there isn't much of a chance to mingle in your area, try hosting your own networking party. There are always ways to get others involved.

Conferences and seminars are also a great way to meet people and build your network. My company tries to attend the American Film Market (AFM) and Screenwriters Expo each year to make new contacts and catch up with people we already know.

Keep in mind to be strategic about your networking activities. Hobnobbing with people outside of your industry or with with people who generally can't help you, is not time well spent. Non-strategic networking will not enhance your career unless that party of insurance brokers wants to purchase your work. Be smart with your time.

The art industry, while fun and inspiring at times, is not known to be an easy industry to break into. You may find that there is a lot of ass-kissing under the guise of appreciation. It's all about who you know and who will be the next greatest thing. Don't let this discourage you. Use your interpersonal skills to your best advantage. Constantly seek out conversations in your industry. Follow-up with your contacts every few months if not to keep yourself fresh in their minds than to update them on your current projects. Additionally, find out what they have been up to you as well. The biggest mistake artists make is to become antisocial. Waiting for people to come to you never works. So, get out there and show them who you are!

I'll risk these cliches to get my point across:

- Walk the walk and talk the talk!
- Say what you mean and mean what you say!

Honesty brings with it a strong character and strong character brings credibility. In any area of business, your credibility is evaluated based on how you fit in, the language you use, the terminology, and (unfortunately or not) looking the part. What you look like and what you say are crucial to selling yourself in any industry. You many find yourself pitching to someone who has been in the business for thirty plus years; they will spot bull-shitters instantly.

Ask yourself:

- What do I want my first impression to be?
- Do I know everything I need to know about what I do?
- Am I going for the black t-shirt of the writer that lives a troubled and tortured life? Or, am I going for the three-piece suit of the city slick modern painter?
- Do I want to be the upbeat, funny person that everybody wants to be around?
- What do I want people to think about once I walk away?

Furthermore, be cognizant of how you are perceived in your chosen group. Now, I know I've made the point that one should avoid looking messy in a professional setting, but there must be room for good judgments when it comes to appearance. For example, I have worked with a lot of musicians in the past. So, I also know how musicians are perceived and what their peers expect from them as a normal look. You would never see the 'talent' showing up to a production meet in a suit. Wearing something so inherently contradictory to your group will definitely raise serious red flags about how firmly entrenched you are in your business. That said, be aware of the norm in your field. And if you're not sure, observe and interact with your peers.

CONFIDENCE BREEDS CONFIDENCE: If you're nervous, act confident and your brain will bring you there. How you walk, talk and make eye contact reveals your confidence level. We have all met the rattled person that stares at the ground, stumbles and fumbles and can't look you in the eye. Think about how you would perceive this character. Do you want to be that person?

MAKE AN IMPRESSION: If you are usually comical, show your true self! It's vitally important to be yourself. Be conscious of how you conduct yourself, for sure, but naturalness and sincerity always makes a good impression.

WORK ON YOUR IMAGE: This doesn't mean spending tons of money on cool clothing, it means presenting your best self. In the same way that you have to develop a brand for your product, you must also develop a brand for yourself.

BE ENGAGING: A desire to engage with others is all it takes to gain a good rapport. To gain respect, listen to what others are saying and engage with them in a humble, interesting way. Conversation is the key to making new friends. Also, be wise to you body language and facial expressions. Folded arms and scowls will communicate that you are not interested in what anyone has to say. Smile, sit and stand with an open posture and witness how much better people react to you.

IN-PERSON MEETINGS

Before you go to an in-person meeting, make sure you have answers to the following questions:

- Do I know what they need?
- Do I know enough about their company?
- How can my work help them?

- What are their goals?
- Can I simplify the sales process for them?

You will have the chance to follow-up with them in a few days in the event that you forget to ask a question. Be prepared for your follow up. Many times, decisions are left to be decided in your client's internal meetings.

If you have made your pitch and there is no answer, you've done your job. Walk away with your head held high. Follow up in a couple days and thank them for their time.

Be patient and learn from each meeting. The most important thing is to emerge knowing that you can't and won't win them all.

Handle rejection professionally and move on to your next client.

Breaking Down the Sale

7 BASIC STEPS

The seven steps of any sale begin after an appointment has been made to make to the party present a traditional sale. Keep in mind these are fundamental sales techniques and, at times, more steps will be needed to close your specific deal.

- Preparation
- Introduction
- Questioning
- Presentation
- Overcoming Objections
- Closing
- Follow up

1. **PREPARATION**

Before you begin, you will conduct research:

- Know about the company thoroughly.

- Know their management structure.

- Know their value structure.

- Get inside information into their office politics

- Know who the decision-makers are.

- Know what their needs are.

2. INTRODUCTION

- Be professional.

- Speak clearly.

- Be totally prepared and have notes to refer to.

- Dress the part.

- Be polite.

- Have your sales pitch memorized and think on your feet.

- Ask if they mind you asking questions.

3. QUESTIONING

The most vital stage is the questioning stage. These questions have to be well thought out in advance.

During Questioning:

- Listen: your biggest job is to listen for the answers.

- Pay attention to body language: understanding theirs and controlling yours.

- Aim your pitch to find their needs or problems: Find out what you can solve.

- Constantly reinforce the win: win mutual benefit from your potential relationship.

- Practice empathy-build trust and rapport by being empathetic to their needs and desires.

- Use open-ended questions that will give you valuable information.

Begin with:

- Who?

- What?
- Why?
- Where?
- When?
- How?

Studies show that utilizing "What?" and "How?" are the most thought-inciting words you can utilize and are also the least threatening.

Do not interrupt: Allow the person to answer. Silence is okay. Many people interrupt a moment of silence and don't let them gather their thoughts; wait for their answer. Choose your words using positivity in your questions.

Don't jump the gun: Wait until you know their need needs and problems. This usually happens towards the end of your discussion, so don't try to solve their problem before it's readily apparent.

4.   PRESENTATION

Your self-presentation and pitch are of central importance in making your prospective clients realize the benefits of working with you and your company. Any good salesperson will take his time with his presentation to match everything the product does to the potential client's needs and wants. The presentation has to demonstrate that your work will solve their quandaries now and well into the future. Market analysis is key to learning as much about the prospective client's company as possible.

All presentations have to be prepared and structured, regardless if it's to schedule a meeting or an impromptu chat at the cafe. Your presentation pitch has to be spot on.

The quality and integrity of your presentation is always a direct indication to the quality of your product and business.

A good presentation will always include past successes, references and testimonials. Re-enforcing that you have solved problems in the past will make your potential customer much more comfortable.

Your presentation should always follow the same style and structure as your audience. Technical people expect a more technical approach, whereas academics might expect a more cerebral approach.

Stay relaxed in your presentation even if you are not. If you don't know the answer to a question, say you are not sure and what you will do to get an answer to them right away.

Don't bash your competition. Harder said than done, taking cheap shots at your competition can actually backfire on you in the long run. Be cautious.

Use props, samples, etc… to get your point across.

Invite questions at the end of your presentation. If you have prepared well enough, you are ready for the objections and concerns they may have.

5.   OVERCOMING OBJECTIONS

Objections will arise, they must be handled calmly and constructively. Always return on the objection professionally and calmly. Many times objections are the result of misunderstanding. Try rephrasing the question. Or, say, "If I hear you correctly, you are saying…."

Objections can also be a simple yearning for more information. Don't take a person's objection or comment personally. A good response might be: "I understand why that could be but, maybe we can work this issue out. Can you tell me more about your concern?" Here are a few other archetypical response you can try:

Deflection: Rephrase the question; this will help you gather your thoughts prior to answering the concern.

Feel-Felt-Found: "I understand how you feel. Have other customers felt the same way?"

At all costs, avoid head-to-head arguments or throwing temper tantrums. This is the fastest way out the door without the sale. Remember to take detailed notes. Even record your meeting if they allow you to do so. When coming to the end of your presentation, don't be shy to ask how you can proceed to work together.

6. CLOSING

Getting to the close in the real art. How you conclude a sale is really a matter of personal style. Relatedly, it is also up to the specific client how they would like to close. Some clients decide quickly, others more cautious will need time to mull it over. Prepare for any of these scenarios. Once you reach that point, close with:

"Are you happy with what we've covered?" and "Would you like to go ahead with this?"

Or, "When would like this delivered?"

It is important to give the customer a nudge toward the actual sale at the end as this small, but imperative step is sometimes overlooked. Ultimately, you have to decide what you're most comfortable with. Here are some additional types of closings:

THE CHALLENGE: "I know most men wouldn't be able to make this purchase without consulting their wife or partner. Do you need their approval?" OR "Most people in your position need to refer this kind of decision to their boss. Do you need to run this by them?"

THE EGO: "I generally find that people with good taste are prepared to pay for the best quality. How you feel about it?"

THE GUILT: "Over three years it may seem like a big purchase, but I find smart business people are willing to invest in their business to improve their bottom line."

THE LAST DITCH: Pack up your materials and prepare to leave at an impasse or elongated silence. You might say: "I obviously failed to portray my work the way I should have. My loss is your loss. Thank you for your time."

THE PROS AND CONS: "I appreciate that money is tight. What normally works is generating a list of pros and cons. Then, you can see the benefits of working with me."

THE PUPPY DOG: "I tell you what, let me leave this with you and take a few days to get used to it. I will wait to hear from you."

7. FOLLOW-UP

The after sale follow-up depends on your product. There are several processes to follow:

- Did you send an order confirmation email?
- Did you set up a delivery date?
- Did you deliver an invoice or COD amount?
- Is your paperwork in order?

Your initial follow-up should be a day or two after the sale is finalized. I would suggest following up every couple of weeks after that to make sure the product is delivered on time and meets all their expectations. Resolve problems immediately to avoid any type of confusion and displeasure with you and your product

CRUCIAL SALES MISTAKES NOT TO MAKE
1. NOT LISTENING

Do not just listen to what the customer is asking for; look past that to find out what they need.

2. OVERSELLING

Eagerness and resoluteness are paramount traits for a salesperson to have, but you must learn how to temper this energy with a cognizance of when an extravagant amount of is an inordinate amount.

3. BEING UNPREPARED

Whether you are making a sale in a showroom, a boardroom, or on the phone, you required knowing the details about what you are selling and being able to answer all pertinent questions.

4. JUMPING STRAIGHT TO THE SALE

In any type of sales business, you are required to establish a relationship. Even on the Web, you require to have landing pages to provide information about your products or accommodations afore jumping to the shopping cart.

5. NOT CLOSING THE SALE

This is the flip side of the above mistake. Once you have provided your customer with the information they require, ask them if they're yare to make a purchase. It may seem nonessential, but sometimes asking for the sale can be the nudge your customer needs to make a final decision.

6. GOING OFF TOPIC

Some salespeople overdo the need for relationship building with excessive chatter.

7. NOT RESEARCHING YOUR CUSTOMER

If you are endeavoring to sell to a certain client at a meeting, you need to know what they are all about. Do some research before the sales meeting and get a good conception of the prospect's needs, company, facility, and manner of doing business.

8. JUDGING BOOKS BY THEIR COVERS

You should approach every sales prospect as a prospective customer. Until you begin to build a relationship with your prospects, you have no idea about their background, needs, or means.

9. NOT FOLLOWING UP ON LEADS

Sometimes, customers need to let things percolate before they are ready to proceed with a sale. Some buyers are impulsive or decisive -- others can be slower to act.

10. FAILING TO PROSPECT FOR NEW CUSTOMERS

Even if you have a full roster of individuals who are current customers and provide you with steady ongoing sales, there are certainly more out there. And you won't know who they are if you don't go looking. Safe to say, they likely won't come looking for you.

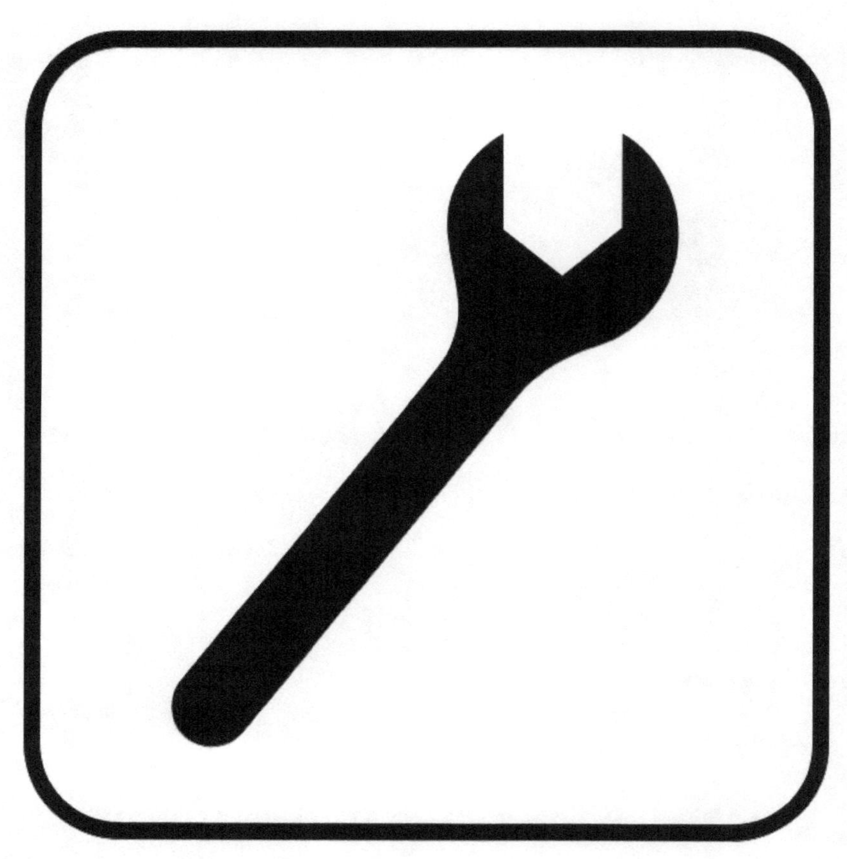

TOOLS

OUTLINES, QUESTIONNAIRES, WORKSHEETS AND SALES SCRIPTS

RESUME REPAIR TOOL

You don't want anything to distract recruiters and hiring managers from your best qualities and qualifications. Take a hard look and give your resume a check-up. Use the following tips to edit your resume to today's acceptable standards:

- Six Immediate Resume Fixes
- You should take the following directly off your resume… right now.

1. "RESPONSIBLE FOR…"

It's obvious that if you accomplished something, then you were responsible for it. This becomes a distraction from your accomplishments. "Responsible for designing supervisory curriculum" is less effective than "Designed supervisory curriculum". The phrase "responsible for" doesn't show anything of value, and, upon seeing it, a hiring manager could mistakenly assume that the entire accomplishment is less important.

2. FORMATTING AND DESIGN

Of course you want your resume to stand out, but it shouldn't be because you chose Comic Sans as your font. Pick a classic format, a common font and be consistent. For example, if you use bullet points and use periods after each point, do that throughout. The hiring manager probably won't waste color ink when printing it and once converted to black and white, your text may appear different than you intended.

3. DATED WORK EXPERIENCE

Any job experience you had ten or more years ago is not relevant to the jobs you will be applying for today.

4. UNPROFESSIONAL EMAIL ADDRESS

If your email provider hasn't been a popular choice for the past several years, you may be subtly communicating to managers and recruiters that you are out of touch. Additionally, try to avoid unprofessional address names. An example of this is a novelty email address might be something like: BritneyNJustinForever@ancientemailprovider.com Avoid names that allude to your personal interests. It is also outdated. Use your common sense.

5.   TOO MUCH INFORMATION ABOUT COLLEGE

Many recent graduates will include information about their fraternity or sorority affiliations on the off chance a recruiter or manager will feel some kinship. This information is just a waste of space. You would be much better off showing off your internships and job experiences. Your GPA is meaningless. It offers no indication of whether you will succeed in the company. The same is true for listing every school you ever attended. The hiring manager doesn't need to know you bounced through three institutions before graduation. Just list the school that's on your diploma.

6.   HOME ADDRESS

At best, this information is unnecessary, and at worst, it can hurt you. If you are looking to relocate, and are applying for positions in other areas of the country, showing your current address can make hiring managers feel like you may not truly be interested or may want relocation assistance that they haven't budgeted for. You will put your address on your formal application and numerous forms once you are hired. It doesn't need to take up valuable real estate on your resume.

TELEPHONE SALES SCRIPTS

PREPARING A TELEPHONE CONTACT SCRIPT

Cold calling is a thankless task; you will get hung up on and insulted. However, a phone call can be an incredibly useful tool to reach out to potential customers and close deals. How can you determine if you have a sales pitch that is effective on the phone?

Use your writing skills to write a customized script that meets your needs.

ELEMENTS OF A TELEPHONE SALES SCRIPT

1. **Introduction:** There always needs to be a polite introduction.
2. **Value Statement:** Grab the prospect's attention, ie. saving them money, increasing sales. That is value that you have to offer.
3. **Disqualify Statement:** A sentence that can help to disarm the person's objections.
4. **Pre-Qualifying Statement:** A few questions to pre-qualify the prospect. Do they have a need? Do they have a budget for your product?
5. **Common Problems:** Share some examples of problems that you have helped other clients through.
6. **Building Interest Points:** List some points to trigger enough interest for you to proceed to the next step in your sales process.
7. **Closing:** Closing is the last step; do not be afraid to ask for their business. Remember that they, too, were in the same position at one time.

ELEMENTS OF A COLD CALL SCRIPT

- Curiosity: Who is this? Why should I care?
- Give context: condensed and concise pitch.
- Ask for permission to continue, or ask if this is a good time.
- Ask questions. What are their needs? How can you help?
- Test close: Mention competitive pricing, or how popular your product has become.
- Schedule next steps.

SAMPLE COLD CALL SCRIPT

Opening:

Hello, my name is___________. I am calling some of the most exciting new startups in the area to find out if they are a good fit for our product.

What we do is [summarize in one sentence] and we provide....

Would this be of any interest to you?

Qualifying:

- What is your current process?
- Who are your customers?
- How do you currently solve x,y,z?

Test Closing:

I hear great things about your company, I would want to start in x weeks—does this work for you? My work is heavily discounted at the moment.. It is going to be $x/per day [or list your pricing structure]. What is the decision making process in your company? Whom do I need to speak with?

Next Steps:

Great. Sounds like this could be a good fit. Let me send you my brochure/website and schedule a time next week to discuss all your questions.What's the best email to send you more information? What's a good time to chat next week?

SAMPLE TELEPHONE SCRIPT #2

Hello, is this [prospect's name]   ? This is Your Name , from Your Company . I'm calling to see if you would be interested in_____________.

If they hang up, then let them. If they say something like, "What are you selling?", ask them a question such as:

That is a good question. Let me give you a quick overview.

OR

Are you looking to grow your business by 30% or more this year?

This attention-getting statement will perk up the ears of your prospects. In essence, use a question that you are sure you will get a YES response. On the off chance you get a NO, let them go; you are wasting your time. If YES...

I'm a [type of service or kind of work you do] and we help people like you to _________________ by helping them _________________.

Ask some more questions to establish their need:

What is the biggest challenge that will slow you down or stop you business from growing?

Make an offer.

Would you like a FREE estimate/consultation/session/?

OR

Would you like a sample perhaps?

Ask for a meeting of some type. REMEMBER: You want a physical meeting, but that may be impossible. A phone appointment is the next best thing. Set up a meeting of 25-minutes.

Offer a FREE consultation of some sort, essentially some free advice. You are the expert here. Very rarely can you sell on your introduction call as you have caught them off guard and unprepared.

Set a time for a FREE meeting: "What is a good day for you to get together this week/next week? I can swing by your office, what's the best time for you?"

You have time to prepare, research the company—who they are and what they do. Then, make the sale!

SIMPLE MARKETING PLAN OUTLINE

NAME:

PRODUCT: Explain the product and what you do.

PRICING: What your price will be per unit.

TARGET AUDIENCE:

- Whom are you selling to?
- Age range?
- Groups?
- Demographics?

DISTRIBUTION

5 or more outlets to sell your product to:

1.
2.
3.
4.
5.
6.

PROMOTION

Where will I advertise—Newspapers, TV, Radio, Web?

    1.

    2.

    3.

    4.

    5.

    6.

GOALS

Top 5 goals for the next 6 months:

    1.

    2.

    3.

    4.

    5.

MARKET RESEARCH CHECKLIST

In this section, you will see what you need to be doing to be on top of what is happening in your industry and with your target market. Check off the points you have done or know the answers to. If there is a point you don't know or understand, highlight it and investigate.

- I know EXACTLY who my target market is.
- I can name my competitors.
- I have compared my pricing to theirs.
- I am on my competitors' mailing and/or email list.
- I know the number of potential customers for my service in my target area.
- I know what the dollar value of the maximum amount of product or service is that I can deliver.
- I have subscribed to marketing and industry information, in the form of email newsletters, print publications or news alerts to stay informed in my industry and marketing in general.
- Now that I am on my competitor's mailing list, I am keeping track of how often my competitors market to me.
- I know the demographics of my ideal customer.
- I have listed the differences I have from my competitors. I know what I actually offer
- Better than my competition and have honestly named what my competition handles better than I do.
- I've had my database of past customers fully analyzed by an outside source, to
- Find commonalities in my customers that may not be obvious from anecdotal data.

DIRECT MAIL

- I have run a mailing list count of my target market.
- My direct mail piece has all necessary design points.

- A clear, bold headline.
- A graphic that supports the message.
- Color that pops.
- Subheads that logically lead into text.
- Benefits, benefits, benefits.

One of the biggest errors people make in advertising is stating features, rather than benefits. For example, never assume potential buyers know what benefit can be derived from a lower interest rate on their mortgage. Let them know that their monthly payments will go down. Remember to include the following:

- A compelling offer.
- Your company name and logo.
- Call to action.
- Contact information.
- Return address.
- A schedule for your direct mail campaign.
- Preparation for receptionists and sales people to receive calls.
- Removal of the returned mail pieces you get from your lists so as not to waste postage.
- Set up a campaign to continually send direct mail pieces to prospects and customers.
- Ran test mailings and made decisions about future campaigns based on the findings.
- Researched how to get the best postage rates.
- Timed direct mail campaigns to correspond with emails and other types of marketing that you are doing.

WEBSITE

- You have a website.

- All of the information on your website is current and accurate.

- Your website has the following:

- A call to action on every page

- A home page that directs visitors exactly where to go

- A place to collect names and contact information with a compelling offer

- Prominent contact information

- A professional design

- An easy-to-navigate menu

- An About Us page with staff pictures

- Testimonials from happy customers

- Photos that support the message you am trying to convey

- An FAQ (Frequently Asked Questions) page if needed

- A Products/Services page that delineates the benefits of each product or service you offer

- Details on any press or awards our company has

- A Contact Us page

Be sure to read through your website from the perspective of a potential customer and ensure that the website is designed to get the viewer to complete an action that you want your visitors to take. (This can also be done by someone who has never been to your site, sit next to them and see where they go and what they click on).

- You have signed up for free local search listings if you have a local business.

- Your website copy is optimized so that search engines will find your site.

- You have video on your site, promoting your product or service.

- You have a blog. (Blog is a combination of the words "web" and "log" meaning that you make regular entries to a specific page.)

- Your website has educational articles and information on it. It is content heavy.

- Your site has a user login area that allows you to track what users do.

- You are using an RSS Feed that pushes content to any users who have signed up to receive it.

- Your blog is updated at least once a week, with search engine friendly posts about timely topics.
- You use Pay-Per-Click marketing, through Google or another provider.

EMAIL MARKETING

- You have tested and determined the best day of the week to send your emails.
- You know how to "split test" two different subject lines.
- You are tracking click through rates, opt out rates and open rates. You use "event triggered" email campaigns.
- You understand how often you should email based on the appropriateness of your subject matter.
- You have set up a system to collect email addresses through your website and over phone.
- You have signed up with an email marketing service.
- You have created a newsletter template which you will update each time you send your newsletter.
- You track responses to your email marketing.

SOCIAL MEDIA

Social Media is a hybrid of marketing and public relations. It should be pursued after basic marketing campaigns have been set up.

- You have an account on Twitter and am building followers.
- You regularly update your profiles on the different networking sites where you are a member.
- You are sending regular messages to your Twitter followers promoting aspects of your business.
- You have hired an outside firm to maintain your pages and profiles across all of the different.
- You have created accounts on Linked In and Facebook.

- You have heard of Twitter, blogger, Word Press, or other smaller networking sites.

TARGETS/BUDGETING

- You set weekly, monthly, and annual leads for generation of targets.

- You keep track of where you are at on these targets and take actions to ensure they are met.

- You know how much it costs to generate one new lead or customer based on past marketing actions.

- You set aside a portion of the money that you make each week for marketing actions.

- You know what the lifetime value of your average customer is so you know how much you want to spend to acquire a new one.

- You have determined what percentage of your gross income you need to set aside for marketing to ensure continued growth.

- You have started building up a reserve to ensure that you can continue your marketing, regardless of the current economic climate.

TRACKING

- You have a notebook or spreadsheet where you will track leads and how they heard about your company.

- Your sales people/receptionists have been trained to ask all prospects how they heard about your company.

- You are tracking the total number of leads from each separate marketing avenue.

- Your are tracking the total revenue from each separate marketing avenue.

- You can calculate your ROI (Return On Expense) from each marketing avenue.

- You have a CRM (Customer Relationship Management) system where you keep track of how contacts heard about your business.

- You are able to pull reports from your CRM system and analyze them.
- You are tracking number of leads from each separate direct mail piece, search term, or specific commercial.
- You actually pull reports from your CRM on a set schedule and make decisions based on what you find.
- You are tracking the channel through which leads are contacting you and calculating most profitable ways people contact you. This means determining if they contacted via phone-call, email, fill out form, or walk-in.

SALES CALL CHECKLIST

1. Preparation Before Sales Call

Checklist: Did you…

- Research the account before the call?
- Learn something about the person and their business before the meeting?
- Send an outline of the agenda to the client before the meeting?
- Have three value-added points prepared?
- Bring all materials, brochures, contracts.

Answer the three important pre-call questions:

- What is the goal of the call?
- What do I need to find out during the call?
- What's the next step after the call?

2. Greeting and Introduction

- Observe the prospect's office décor (e.g., trophies, awards, pictures, etc).
- Find out about the prospect's personal interests, hobbies, family, etc.
- Find out the names of contacts in the account and write them down.
- Segue to the business topic smoothly.
- Listen more than you speak. Ideally, you should spend 80% of your time listening and only 20% talking.

- Ask the customer about their business goals

- Ask the customer what challenges the company is facing

3. Qualifying

- Find out whom the decision-makers are by asking: "Who else beside yourself might be involved in the decision making process?"

- Ask what process they normally go through when considering a new vendor.

- Find out how and why they made the decision for their current product or service (assuming they are replacing a product or service).

- Find out what their time frame is.

- Find out if funds have been allocated and how much.

- Find out their specific needs.

- Ask if they could change something about their product or service, what would it   be?

4. Surveying

- Ask open-ended questions— Who, What, Where, When, Why, How, How much, Describe it for me?

- Ask about the corporate structure.

- Ask about the prospect's role at the company.

- Ask what's important to them.

- Ask what's interesting to them and then focus on that.

- Ask what risks they perceive.

- Ask how you can help solve their problems.

- Ask what they think about your company.

- Ask what they like and dislike about their current vendor.

- Ask how industry trends are affecting them.

- Ask "What if?" questions.

- Ask what they would like to see from a vendor and salesperson in the area of support after the sale.

- Ask what their short-term and long-term goals are.

- Ask how you can become their most valued vendor.
- Ask: "What is the next step?"
- Establish a specific follow-up schedule.
- Parrot the prospect to encourage him to expand, elaborate, and go into detail about each answer.

5. **Handling Objections**

- Listen to the entire objection.
- Pause for three seconds before responding.
- Remain calm and do not get defensive.
- Meet the objection with a question in order to find out more.
- Restate the objection to make sure you both agreed. Effective communication is key.
- Answer the objection.
- Complete the six-step process:
    1. Listen
    2. Define
    3. Rephrase
    4. Isolate
    5. Present solution
    6. Close (or next step)

6. **Presentation**

- Prioritize the prospect's needs.
- Talk about benefits to the customer.
- Used easy terms.
- Link the benefit to the prospect's needs.
- Verify each need before moving on.
- Present company, product, and yourself in a positive light.
- Re-establish a good rapport.
- Ask if anything changed since your last meeting.
- Pre-commit the prospect.
- Give a general overview of the product or service.

- Keep the presentation focused on the customer's needs.

- Involve the customer in the presentation.

- Summarize the prospect's needs and how your product or service meets those needs.

7. Closing

- Get the customer to identify all possible problems that might be solved by your product or service.

- Get the customer to identify the value of solving the identified problems.

- Get agreement that the proposed solution provides the values identified?

- Ask for the order, i.e. "Why don't we go ahead with this?"

8. Customer Maintenance

- Write "Thank You" letters for appointments, orders, and so on.

- Earn the right to ask for reference letters and referrals.

- Establish a schedule for follow-up calls and customer visits.

- Ask for referrals: "Do you know three people who could benefit from my product and service like you did?"

- Send "Thank You" notes to lost accounts.

- Ask for three important things you do as a vendor to keep your relationship strong.

TARGET MARKET DEMOGRAPHIC CHECKLIST
QUESTIONNAIRE

1. How old is your target customer? (Check all that apply)

- 17 or younger   [ ]
- 18-20   [ ]
- 21-29   [ ]
- 30-39   [ ]
- 40-49   [ ]
- 50-59   [ ]
- 60-64   [ ]
- 65 or older   [ ]

2.   What gender is your target customer?

- Male   [ ]
- Female   [ ]
- Both male and female   [ ]

3.   What is the highest level of education your target customer has completed or the highest degree they have achieved? (Check all that apply)

- Less than high school diploma   [ ]
- High school diploma or equivalent (e.g.GED)   [ ]
- Some college but no degree   [ ]
- Associate degree   [ ]
- Bachelor degree   [ ]
- Graduate degree   [ ]
- PhD   [ ]

4.   Which of the following categories best describes your target customer's employment status? (Check all that apply)

- Employed, working 1-39 hours per week   [ ]
- Employed, working 40 or more hours per week   [ ]
- Not employed, looking for work   [ ]
- Not employed, NOT looking for work   [ ]
- Retired   [ ]
- Disabled, not able to work   [ ]

5.   Which of the following best describes your target customer's current occupation? (Check all that apply)

- Installation, Maintenance, and Repair   [ ]
- Arts, Design, Entertainment   [ ]
- Sports   [ ]
- Media   [ ]
- Life, Physical, and Social Science   [ ]
- Office and Administrative Support   [ ]
- Business and Financial Operations   [ ]
- Healthcare Practitioners   [ ]

- Technical, Computer, and Mathematical [ ]
- Community and Social Services [ ]
- Healthcare Support [ ]
- Education, Training, and Library [ ]
- Production [ ]
- Building, Grounds, Cleaning, Landscaping, Maintenance [ ]
- Legal [ ]
- Government, Law Enforcement [ ]
- Architecture and Engineering [ ]
- Management [ ]
- Construction and Extraction [ ]
- Farming, Fishing, and Forestry [ ]
- Sales and Related [ ]
- Food Preparation and Serving Related [ ]
- Protective Service [ ]
- Personal Care and Service [ ]
- Transportation and Materials Moving [ ]
- Other (please specify) [ ]

6. What is your target customer's yearly household income? (Check all that apply)

- Less than $20,000 [ ]
- $20,000 to $34,999 [ ]
- $35,000 to $49,999 [ ]
- $50,000 to $74,999 [ ]
- $75,000 to $99,999 [ ]
- $100,000 to $149,999 [ ]
- $150,000 to $199,999 [ ]
- $200,000 or more [ ]

7. What is your target customer's marital status? (Check all that apply)

- Widowed [ ]
- Married [ ]
- Separated [ ]

- Divorced [ ]
- Never married   [ ]

8.   Does your target customer have children?

- Yes, they do   [ ]
- No, they do not   [ ]
- They may or may not   [ ]

9.   How old are your target customer's children? (Check all that apply)

- Less than 1 year old   [ ]
- 2 - 4 years old   [ ]
- 5 - 7 years old   [ ]
- 8 - 10 years old   [ ]
- 11 - 13 years old   [ ]
- 14 - 16 years old   [ ]
- 16 - 17 years old   [ ]
- 18 years old or older   [ ]

10.   What is your target market's living situation?

- Owned or being bought by them or someone in their household   [ ]
- Rented with cash   [ ]
- Occupied without payment of cash rent [ ]

11.   Does your target customer own a business or a farm?

- Yes, they do   [ ]
- No, they do not   [ ]
- Some may and some may not   [ ]

12.   In what city (or cities) does your target customer live?

13.   In what states or U.S. territories does your target customer live? (Check all that apply)

- Alabama [ ]
- Alaska   [ ]
- American Samoa   [ ]
- Arizona   [ ]
- Arkansas [ ]

- California [ ]
- Colorado [ ]
- Connecticut [ ]
- Delaware [ ]
- District of Columbia (DC) [ ]
- Florida [ ]
- Georgia [ ]
- Guam [ ]
- Hawaii [ ]
- Idaho [ ]
- Illinois [ ]
- Indiana [ ]
- Iowa [ ]
- Kansas [ ]
- Kentucky [ ]
- Louisiana [ ]
- Maine [ ]
- Maryland [ ]
- Massachusetts [ ]
- Michigan [ ]
- Minnesota [ ]
- Mississippi [ ]
- Missouri [ ]
- Montana [ ]
- Nebraska [ ]
- Nevada [ ]
- New Hampshire [ ]
- New Jersey [ ]
- New Mexico [ ]
- New York [ ]
- North Carolina [ ]

- North Dakota [ ]
- Northern Marianas Islands [ ]
- Ohio [ ]
- Oklahoma [ ]
- Oregon [ ]
- Pennsylvania [ ]
- Puerto Rico [ ]
- Rhode Island [ ]
- South Carolina [ ]
- South Dakota [ ]
- Tennessee [ ]
- Texas [ ]
- Utah [ ]
- Vermont [ ]
- Virginia [ ]
- Virgin Islands [ ]
- Washington [ ]
- West Virginia [ ]
- Wisconsin [ ]
- Wyoming[ ]

14. In what type of community does your target customer live? (Check all that apply)

- City or urban community [ ]
- Suburban community [ ]
- Rural community [ ]
- Other (please specify) [ ]

15. . In which type of housing does your target customer live? (Check all that apply)

- Military housing [ ]
- Townhouse [ ]
- Apartment [ ]

- Mobile home   [ ]
- Condominium   [ ]
- Houseboat   [ ]
- Duplex   [ ]
- Single-family house   [ ]
- Other (please specify) [ ]

16. Who lives with your target customer? (Check all that apply)

- Parent   [ ]
- Roommate   [ ]
- Nobody   [ ]
- Child   [ ]
- Grandchild   [ ]
- Grandparent   [ ]
- Romantic partner (spouse, partner, boyfriend, girlfriend, etc.)   [ ]
- Other (please specify)   [ ]

17. What race is your target customer? (Check all that apply)

- White   [ ]
- African-American [ ]
- American Indian or Alaskan Native Asian   [ ]
- Native Hawaiian or other Pacific Islander   [ ]
- Some other race (please specify)   [ ]

18. Is your target customer Spanish, Hispanic, or Latino?

- Yes, they are   [ ]
- No, they are not   [ ]
- Some may be and some may not be   [ ]

19. If you target customer is Latin, what region are they from? (Check all that apply)

- Mexican [ ]
- Mexican-American [ ]
- Chicano [ ]
- Puerto Rican   [ ]

- Cuban [ ]
- Cuban-American [ ]
- Some other Spanish, Hispanic, or Latino group (please specify) [ ]

20. Is your target customer currently serving in the United States military, or not?

- Yes, they are [ ]
- No, they are not [ ]

21. In which branch (or branches) of the United States military has your target customer served? (Check all that apply)

- Marine Corps [ ]
- Navy [ ]
- Army [ ]
- Air Force [ ]
- Coast Guard [ ]
- National Guard [ ]

22. Does your target customer subscribe to a religion? (Check all that apply)

- Muslim [ ]
- Christian [ ]
- Jewish [ ]
- Buddhist [ ]
- Hindu [ ]
- Wiccan [ ]
- A follower of some other religion [ ]
- Not religious [ ]

23. What is your target market's sexual orientation? (Check all that apply)

- Heterosexual [ ]
- Homosexual [ ]
- Bisexual [ ]
- Asexual [ ]
- Pansexual [ ]
- Transsexual [ ]
- Something else (please specify) [ ]

24. What is your target market's primary language? (Check all that apply)

- Arabic   [ ]
- Armenian[ ]
- Chinese [ ]
- English [ ]
- French   [ ]
- French Creole [ ]
- German   [ ]
- Greek   [ ]
- Gujarati   [ ]
- Hindi   [ ]
- Italian   [ ]
- Japanese [ ]
- Korean   [ ]
- Persian   [ ]
- Polish   [ ]
- Portuguese   [ ]
- Russian [ ]
- Spanish [ ]
- Tagalo   [ ]
- Urdu   [ ]
- Vietnamese   [ ]
- Other (please specify) [ ]

25. In what languages can your target customer speak? (Check all that apply)

- Arabic   [ ]
- Armenian[ ]
- Chinese [ ]
- English [ ]
- French   [ ]
- French Creole [ ]
- German   [ ]

- Greek   [ ]
- Gujarati   [ ]
- Hindi   [ ]
- Italian   [ ]
- Japanese [ ]
- Korean   [ ]
- Persian   [ ]
- Polish   [ ]
- Portuguese   [ ]
- Russian   [ ]
- Spanish   [ ]
- Tagalo   [ ]
- Urdu   [ ]
- Vietnamese   [ ]
- Other (please specify) [ ]

EVENT PLANNING QUESTIONNAIRE

1. Will you be attending this event?

   Yes [ ]   No [ ]

2. If you will not be attending this event, please explain why:

3. How did you hear about this event?

4. How easy was the registration process for this event?

- Extremely easy [ ]
- Quite easy [ ]
- Moderately easy [ ]
- Slightly easy [ ]

- Not at all easy [ ]

5. Do you have any dietary restrictions?

6. Who will be paying you to attend this event?

7. What topics would you most like to learn about or discuss at this event?

8. Are there any questions you would like to be addressed at this event?

9. Are there any questions you would like to be addressed by the speaker at this event?

10. How would you like to receive additional information regarding this event?

   - Email [ ]
   - Phone [ ]
   - Mail   [ ]
   - Other (Please Specify) [ ]

COMPLETE MARKETING CHECKLIST

You don't need to develop all of these tools, but I would suggest developing some in each category. That way, you have a balanced marketing approach.

Write Y or N in the lists below:

1. **BRAND YOURSELF**

Branding yourself means getting your name out there and associated with something specifically related to what you offer; it is not merely name recognition. The minute they think of you, they think of what you offer. Three key aspects of branding are:

1. **Name for my business practice that helps promote me instantly:**
- I need? ___
- I am using? ___
- It works? ___
- Did not work. ____
2. **Logo/Graphics**
- I need? ___

- I am using? ___
- It works? ___
- Did not work. ____

3. 30-Second Commercial

- I need? ___
- I am using___
- It works? ___
- Did not work. ____

2. PROMOTIONAL PACKAGE/MEDIA KIT

You never know when you'll need to send information to the media. Here are the essential elements:

1. Biographical profile

- I need? ___
- I am using? ___
- It works? ___
- Did not work. ____

2. Biographical feature story (highlight yourself or, even better, highlight the way you helped a client)

- I need? ___
- I am using? ___
- It works? ___
- Did not work. ____

3. Business description & history

- I need? ___
- I am using? ___
- It works? ___
- Did not work. ____

4. Brochure(s)

- I need? ___

- I am using? ___
- It works? ___
- Did not work. ____

5. **Fact Sheet/Product-Service description**

- I need? ___
- I am using___
- It works? ___
- Did not work. ____

6. **News Release/Media Advisory (mistakenly called a Press Release.)**

- I need? ___
- I am using? ___
- It works? ___
- Did not work. ____

3. **ATTRACTION TOOLS**

In marketing, you go out and aggressively tell people what you offer. Attraction is a more indirect way of bringing clients and customers to you based on their getting to know you and valuing you. You have to offer MASSIVE value to people in the attraction approach (for free or cheap), and then they'll trust you enough to spend significant money for even more value. Some key attraction tools:

Newsletter (email or print or both)

- I need? ___
- I am using? ___
- It works? ___
- Did not work. ____

Booklets or Special Reports

- I need? ___
- I am using? ___

- It works? ___
- Did not work. ___

Free Trials (e.g. consultations, e-book, software)

- I need? ___
- I am using? ___
- It works? ___
- Did not work. ___

Take-ones

These are small cards with a brief article on them that you can place in church vestibules, doctors' offices, store counters, etc.

- I need? ___
- I am using? ___
- It works? ___
- Did not work. ___

4. ADVERTISING

Advertising is a more direct method of getting to people who might buy from you or hire you. You can ADVERTISE TO SELL in which case you want your ad to motivate, or you can ADVERTISE TO GENERATE INTEREST. We call this "lead generation advertising" because you offer people a reason to raise their hands and say, "I am potentially interested in your product or service." Offering a free report is often a good technique for this two-step advertising approach.

Classified Ads (online or off)

- I need? ___
- I am using? ___
- It works? ___
- Did not work. ___

Display/Space Ads

- I need? ___
- I am using? ___
- It works? ___
- Did not work. ____

Article Ads

Write an article that is actually an ad. This is not the same as sending articles around. Some people call this an advertorial.

- I need? ___
- I am using? ___
- It works? ___
- Did not work. ____

Yellow Pages Ads

- I need? ___
- I am using? ___
- It works? ___
- Did not work. ____

Directory Listings/Ads

- I need? ___
- I am using? ___
- It works? ___
- Did not work. ____

5. DIRECT MAIL

Direct mail is when you send a letter or package of materials to prospects. It is quite effective for professionals and small business people to use if done properly.

1-2 page letters

- I need? ___
- I am using? ___
- It works? ___
- Did not work. ___

Long form sales letters

(4+ pages, usually 4 - 12)

- I need? ___
- I am using? ___
- It works? ___
- Did not work. ___

Postcards (including card decks)

- I need? ___
- I am using? ___
- It works? ___
- Did not work. ___

Flyers

- I need? ___
- I am using? ___
- It works? ___
- Did not work. ___

Faxes

Outgoing to current customers or interested people. In the U.S., it's illegal to send fax ads to people who haven't demonstrated interest— like spamming but illegal.

- I need? ___
- I am using? ___
- It works? ___
- Did not work. ____

Fax-On-Demand

People call a number from their fax machine and receive back your sales letter. Not as much use these days in the U.S.

- I need? ___
- I am using? ___
- It works? ___
- Did not work. ____

6.   OTHER PRINT TOOLS

There are many times when you'll want to have other things to give to people. The more creative they are the better, but no need to spend money. Human interest stories are best, especially client success stories. Also good are checklists and self-assessment "Test Your Emotional IQ" type guides. Use your imagination.

Business Cards

Most people don't use business cards properly. Think of them more like space ads, but slightly modified.

- I need? ___
- I am using? ___
- It works? ___

- Did not work. _____

Tear Pads

(May go with flyers)

- Developed? ___
- I am using? ___
- Effective? __

Coupons

Yes you can use these as a professional tool in the right marketing campaign. You can certainly use them with products. Some services can have an "After 3 sessions the 4th one is free" approach. Instead of just saying it, check off each visit on a coupon, and then redeem the coupon on the 4th visit.

- I need? ___
- I am using? ___
- It works? ___
- Did not work. _____

Gift Certificates

Ditto above. Give your services as a gift.

- I need? ___
- I am using? ___
- It works? ___
- Did not work. _____

Inserts

Used in fusion marketing. If you know what that is, great. If not, it is like a joint venture.

- I have? ___
- I am using? ___
- It works? ___
- Did not work. ____

Proposals

You definitely want to know how to develop proposals if you offer services, both for private contracts and the government. It is best to develop templates you can quickly modify.

- I have? ___
- I am using? ___
- It works? ___
- Did not work. ____

7.   ONLINE TOOLS

Website With Heavy Content

- I need? ___
- I am using? ___
- It works? ___
- Did not work. ____

Email Marketing Tools

These might include blogs, newsletter, or email promotions.

- I need? ___
- I am using? ___
- It works? ___
- Did not work. ____

Banner Ads

Overall, you can use this to market your SITE but, not directly to your services. Banner ad effectiveness is slowly decreasing, but still viable at times.

- I need? ___
- I am using? ___
- It works? ___
- Did not work. ___

8.   TELEPHONE TOOLS

Answering Machine/Voicemail

Yes, you're answering message should sell people on your products and services if prospects call your number a lot. You can use a soft sell if you'd like, but a name and a generic message like, "I am away from my desk" message are useless.

- I need?___
- I am using__
- It works?___
- Did not work. ___

Voice-on-demand system

Like a fax-on-demand, but with voice messages that people can listen to.

- I need? ___
- I am using? ___
- It works? ___
- Did not work. ___

Telephone script for outgoing calls

If you do cold calling or any sales calls, you definitely want a script or two.

- I need? ___
- I am using? ___

- It works? ___
- Did not work. ____

9. OTHER POTENTIAL TOOLS

The tools below are just a small sample of the additional approaches you may want to consider.

Conference booth displays. If you go to conferences, you MUST not only have a good display, you must also have good ways to get people's names and addresses, like giving away something for free— and NOT a pen or ruler!

- I need? ___
- I am using? ___
- It works? ___
- Did not work. ____

Radio Ads

You can also consider paying for a half-hour interview in a studio as a kind of radio infomercial. Then, buy airtime on various stations in your area. This is VERY effective for professional marketing services. It allows you to maintain a very professional image.

- I need? ___
- I am using? ___
- It works? ___
- Did not work. ____

Computer Disks

In other words, an electronic book you can hand out or mail. Internet downloads are only partially effective right now.

- I need? ___
- I am using? ___
- It works? ___

- Did not work. _____

SALES PROMOTION CHECKLIST

1. What is the objective? Is it to secure new leads, or is it to win over customers from your competitors?

2. What product/service should you discount to achieve this objective? Will it be a high-value or low-value item? Will it be a specialty item or one that appeals to the masses?

3. Do you need market research to ensure this promotion appeals to your targeted audience? Can you trial run the promotion first with a select number of clients from your customer base?

4. How will these types of sales promotions impact your branding? Will you be cheapening your brand? Will you be encouraging brand loyalty?

5. When will the promotion be considered a success? How much do you have to sell to cover the work you put in and the reduction in your margin to make an acceptable profit?

6. Have you assessed the risks? Will you run out of product (do you need to limit the numbers for this promotion)? Is the success of this promotion within your capacity, in regards to people or otherwise? What happens if your competitors match or better your promotion? What happens if it flops? How can you change the proposition if the market doesn't take up the offer?

7. What are your secondary goals, beyond simply increasing sales? Can you increase your database of lead and customer contacts? Can you increase awareness of your brand? Anything else?

8. How will you measure the effectiveness of the campaign? You need to develop a marketing register to monitor your return on investment, and you need to monitor what did and didn't work for next time, because if it is a success, you will want to do it again!

Now you need to move on to the tactical decisions. How are you going to promote this sales campaign? Below are some suggestions you can implement:

- Develop specific communication messages

- Provide sales staff training, sales scripts, and sales incentives

- Include an end date to add urgency and prompt people into action

- Harness your database of contacts

- Use traditional advertising mediums

- Take advantage of your affiliate and collaborate relationships

- Promote it on your website

- Print specific marketing collateral

- Write press releases and explore other PR opportunities

- Promote it through social media

- Use direct marketing – e-newsletter, sales email, mail outs, etc.

- Do everything within your means (and budget) to reach your objectives without harming your brand!

PRE-LAUNCH CHECKLIST AND TASKS

- Write sales copy for website.

- Write sales copy for email.

- Write sales copy for affiliates (if applicable).

- Write Tweets and social media posts.

- Have a graphic design for the product/service.

- Set up shopping cart buttons with "Thank You" text.

- Set up discount codes (if applicable).

- Set up landing page on website.

- Test landing page and purchase process, including product download link and email responders

- Write related blog posts to promote new product/service.

- Schedule blog posts to publish.

- Schedule social media promotions.

- Schedule email announcement(s) to mailing list.

- Reach out to affiliates/J.V. partners.

LAUNCH DAY TASKS

- Schedule the full day at your desk.
- Double-check landing page and purchase process.
- Announce to social media networks if not already scheduled.
- Announce to online groups and forums.
- Send a press release (if applicable).
- Send reminder emails to J.V. partners.
- Report progress on social media networks throughout the day to build momentum.
- Monitor email for questions or issues throughout the day.

POST-LAUNCH DAY TASKS

- Use email reminders for any important dates, open houses or sales.
- Use social media networks to make people aware of important dates.
- Respond quickly to your audience and followers.
- Make notes as to what event worked and what didn't. Make adjustments accordingly.

YOUR STRATEGY

This is a bit of a "chicken and the egg" situation. You may need to cull through and validate your responses to these questions as you uncover more information through the preparation process.

- Where is the buyer in their decision-making process?
- Where are you in your selling process?
- What are the objectives for your call?
- What information, support, or decisions do you need to achieve your objectives?

BREAKING DOWN THE BUYER

What's going on in the buyer's company?

- At the point where you can attach your proficiencies to an organization's key activities, you stand a good shot of getting official consideration.

- Let's look at Google for a moment: Go to your computer and open Google in your browser. In the search field, type a company name of your choosing. Click on a few links to see what's going on. Have there been any "trigger events"? Try Googling the phrases <[company name] problems> and <[company name] strategy>.

- If the company you chose to research is publicly traded, visit the investor relation's site and watch recordings of their recent CEO's analyst presentations.

- If the company is private equity (PE) owned, visit the PE firm's website to learn about their investment strategy and philosophy.

- Also, identify the Principle at the PR firm responsible for your target company.

What's going on in the buyer's industry?

- It is my personal belief that if you want to be successful in selling to sophisticated buyers, you need to develop expertise in the buyer's industry. Staying current on industry trends should be a continuous process.

- Research other companies in the industry. Once you establish and develop your CRM, be sure to refer back to your system to see related work you may have done.

- Google "Recent challenges in the <insert buyer's industry> industry".

- Google "Top issues facing <insert buyer's role>".

- Google "Top issues facing <enter buyer's role> in the < insert buyer's industry> industry"

- Google "<insert client's industry> industry associations"

- Google "<insert client's industry> industry study"

- Google "<McKinsey, Deloitte, BCG, Bain, PWC, KPMG, E&Y...> industry report"

What's going on in the buyer's career and life?

- It is always better to relate to your buyer on a personal level. We live in a world of information overload, spam email, and automated messaging. Mass messaging falls on deaf ears.
- Connect with the buyer on Linked In and follow them if they are active there, on Twitter, or some other social media platform.
- Google "<buyer's name, title and company>", and pay attention not only to what is happening in their business life but in their personal life as well.
- See if the buyer has spoken on YouTube or shared presentations on SlideShare.
- See if the buyer is active in associations or has presented at conferences.
- See if the buyer is active on any blog platforms.
- See if you have any mutual connections on Linked In, and reach out to any connections you believe would be willing to share insight to help you understand the buyer better.

Who else will influence the buying process?

- Try to learn in advance who will influence the decision-making process to buy from you. People have a tendency to link to their colleagues on Linked In, some of whom you can infer will be influential.
- See whom the buyer is linked to on Linked In. Many people have a tendency to link to colleagues and others in their functional area.
- Visit each buying influence Linked In profile and pay close attention to whether he or she are linked to any of your competitors. If they are, this is a red flag.

SAMPLE SALES & MARKETING LETTERS

Sample Letter #1

I HAVE SOME IMPORTANT NEWS TO BOLSTER YOUR FALL SALES! The shipment has finally arrived!

Our new line of DVD players is here! You can begin ordering today.

This advanced technology has been widely publicized, and we have been bombarded with inquiries. "When can we get them?" "Our customers are waiting for them." The waiting is over. Your customers will be delighted to know that these DVD players can be in your store within days.

The enclosed literature describes all the features. Your discount schedule is also included. Take a careful look. You'll see that by just ordering a few more players, your profit margin increases dramatically. In addition, you can also qualify for a special discount of 3% on orders placed before September 30.

Hurry and place your order today. We guarantee a 48-hour turnaround. You don't want to leave your customers out in the cold.

Sample Letter #2

Delinquent accounts taking too much of your time and money?

Many corporations have discovered that in-house collections—staff, telephone calls, invoicing, collections letters—are costing them more than the effort is worth. In fact, they find that their collection department actually loses money.

Our professional collection agency can handle every detail of your collections and recover more money at a lower cost.

That is what we guarantee. Collections are our business. During our 20 years in the collection business, we have refined a successful system that produces exceptional results. What's more, is that there is no fee for this service. We only take a percentage of what we collect. If we don't collect, we aren't paid!

Please review the list of companies that use our service. Call them and ask about our efficiency. Their satisfaction is a better endorsement than we could ever give.

We have a special introductory offer for you: Try us out for three months at half our regular percentage rate. To receive this special price, you must mail in the enclosed card within two weeks. After October 31, this special offer will no longer be available.

Act today. We look forward to helping you collect more of the money that is owed you.

P.S. Our customers realize an average 40% increase over their own collection efforts in the first 30 days! We can do the same for you!

Sample Letter #3

The holiday season is fast approaching. Let me help you save time shopping for gifts.

I carry a unique gift line that is both historic and beautiful. I have hundreds of specimens of Dominican amber with insects. Additionally, I carry Dominican blue amber with and without insects.

Many of my customers also purchase a loupe to get a closer view at those insects in the amber. When you buy amber from me, I will discount the loupe 25%!

Here are some of the things people are saying about my amber:

(List testimonials)

A full display of photographs and pricing can be found on my website (list web address), or you can call me at (Phone number). I'll be happy to answer your questions.

Sample Letter #4

Downy Draperies congratulates you on the purchase of your new home! This event represents not only a significant achievement, but also an exciting adventure. With a new home comes the excitement of decorating it according to you own tastes, and Downy Draperies is prepared to help with a full line of blinds and window coverings.

Call us at 555-5555 or drop by our showroom at 1600 Main Street in downtown Springfield to arrange for one of our interior decorators to visit your home for a free consultation. There is no obligation to buy, but we are certain you will like our beautiful selection.

Sample Letter #5

Shop by catalog and save time and money! The prices of these beautiful suits and dresses consistently rival those in retail stores. Say goodbye to hasty purchases at the end of a long day. No more tired legs and feet. Relax! Let your eyes enjoy a walk through the pages and do your shopping at great savings.

All of our clothes are made of high-quality wool, velour, silk, and rayon, and all are made in the USA. Our sizes range from petite to extra-large with three different lengths (petite, medium, tall) for each pant size. With this introductory offer, we are slashing our already low prices by an incredible 30%.

Our service offers one-day delivery, low shipping costs, and full, immediate refunds if you are not satisfied. So, give your feet a break and enjoy shopping in the comfort of your own home. When you are ready to order, call our toll-free number at 1-800-555-5555.

Sample "Thank You" Letter

In honor of Mother's Day, The Doe Corporation pays special tribute to the hard-working women in our company. We know of the challenges you face balancing work and family responsibilities. We salute you and thank you for all you do. Please accept this book of verse by our favorite women poets as a small token of our appreciation. Have a wonderful Mother's Day!

Follow-up Sample Letter #1

Thank you for allowing me to show you the floor plans for homes we intend to build this summer. These homes are an exceptional value, with spacious bedrooms, high ceilings, and versatile family rooms. Remember that with a $500 down payment you can lock in your price and reserve your lot. With today's rapidly escalating costs, you realize how important this offer is. For a full 30 days, your check is completely refundable. You have nothing to lose and a lovely home to gain. Call and we will help you find the home you've been dreaming of but never imagined was within your grasp.

Follow up- Sample Letter #2

Thanks for taking the time to meet with me last (day). I think you will agree that we had a very productive meeting. During our meeting, we spoke about your company's need for twice-weekly deliveries. We also spoke about my company's ability to provide these deliveries with a two-hour advance notice. The following points summarize our discussion:

(list points of discussion)

Over the next few days, I will draft a formal proposal, which will address these points. When the proposal is ready for your review, I will call you to set up an appointment for a formal presentation. In the meantime, if you have any questions, please call me at 555-5555.

Thanks again for your time and consideration.

Follow up- Sample Letter #3

During our last meeting, we came to some preliminary decisions about working together. I believe I have a good understanding of your needs and you have a clear view of my services.

Therefore, I am asking that we sign a simple Letter of Intent so we can move toward a final contract. This letter would state your intent to contract with me and to make payments according to the schedule I described in my proposal to you. Once we sign this Letter of Intent, I will begin to process the final contract.

I will call you at the end of this week to set up an appointment to sign a Letter of Intent. I look forward to working with you.

GLOSSARY OF TERMS

A.B.C- Abbreviation for (always be closing)

Above the Line Advertising-Commission payable to the agency that represents you. This includes TV, print, magazine.

Active Listening

The active listener studies the words said but someone else. The active listener is listening for keywords that will help them fix their problem.

Adoption Process

Any buying method for first-time purchases, particularly regarding consumer markets and composed of: Awareness, Awareness, Evaluation, Demo, Adoption, Post-Adoption conformation: much like AIDA

Advertising

The activity of attracting public attention to a product or business by paid announcements in print, broadcast and electronic media.

Agent

The agent represents the artist, and sell to buyers. The artist who is the owner of the goods pays the agent a commission. They do not take title, or ownership, of the goods.

AIDA

Attention, Interest, Desire, Action: a marketing model describing the stages that promotion can take a target audience through: is often used to set promotional objectives

Alternative Close

There are several alternative close options. An alternative close is used when the traditional close appears not to be working.

Assumption/Assumptive Close

This is where the salesperson works on the assumption that it's a "done deal" and they just need to iron out the finer points. It should be used carefully as it making assumptions can annoy the buyer.

Ambient Media

Also known as 'Fringe media'. It includes different sources of advertising not in the mainstream such as billboards, banners, ballpark advertising, buses and the like.

B

Barter

Barter is an exchange of good and services in exchange for other goods and services. Example a mechanic may barter his time to fix your car in exchange for someone to paint his garage.

Behavioral Segmentation

A way of classifying people into separate groups. Identifying segments of people that use a product in a certain way.

Below the Line

Public relations, sales promotions, direct mail, point of sale. All promotional advertising. These services (which agencies are not paid commission).

Benefit

The value of the product or service experienced by the consumer. The benefit is the basis for the sale. Than the feature are added on top of the benefits to the buyer.

Body Language

Non verbal communication method and includes the way you stand or sit, facial expressions, gesticulations, how you hold your head and use your eyes

Brand

A name, term, design, symbol or any other feature that identifies one seller's good or service as distinct from those of other sellers.

Brand Extension

A strategy whereby a firm uses an existing brand name for a new product to be marketed to the same market. A good example of this is Coke than all the other Coke brands that spun off from Coke.

Broker

An intermediary who tends to trade on behalf of the customer, rather than the principal and so will tend to have agreements with many principal organizations. The broker can and does work with several different clients at one time.

Business Plan

A formal well written document that outlines the mission, who you are, what you do, how you attend to get to your desired goals and how you measure success.

Business to Business (B2B)

One business selling to another business their goods or services in exchange change into another product or service. This is (B2B) rather than a consumer buying for personal consumption or (B2C).

Business to Consumer (B2C)

Is where a business sells directly to consumers. Products or service are used for personal use rather than business use.

Business Buyer Behavior

The buying process and factors that influence the process when businesses purchase goods or services.

Buyer

The person that makes the purchasing decision. The buyer has the authority to say yes or no to purchasing.

Buying Criteria

A written, or unwritten, checklist of the requirements of the purchaser when making a buying decision egg price, speed of delivery, quality and so on

Buying signal

A formal or informal request to move ahead with the closing process. The buying signal is the time that the salesperson knows the buyer is serious and willing to purchase.

C

Call center

Call centers are based around the world. A call center is a large office set up with telephones and qualified people to answers questions and concerns regarding a product or service.

Cash Cows

This is business slang for a product generates a steady income beating expectations and making its money back plus profits.

Canvas

Another term in searching for new prospects to sell your product or service to. Canvassing can be done in person on the telephone or through email.

Cash and Carry

A business that does not use credit. Cash and carry is what it says; pay cash and carry away the product.

Channel of Distribution

The channels of distribution are where a product must travel to get to its destination for purchase. Different products have different channels to travel. Some include, Inspection, quality control, product testing and the like.

Closed Questions

Closed questions are used in marketing research. The questions are in the form of a questionnaire, and provide optional answers to each question. They are questions where all the possible answers are provided by the researcher, usually on a questionnaire, enabling the respondent to choose between a yes or no answer.

Closed Gestures

Body language is the signal for closed gestures. Arms crossed, looking at the ceiling, not paying attention. These gestures signal that the person you are speaking to is closed to your ideas or communication.

Closing Questions

The closing question are crucial to complete the sale. Closing question solidify to the buyer that they have made the correct choice working with you. Closing questions are designed to get the buyer to say yes.

Closing (The Sale)

The close is the final and most important step in the sale. This is where the salesperson ask for the buyers business. There are a few different techniques to closing. The Alternative Close, Direct Close, Cautious Close and Assumptive Close, to name a few.

Cold Calling

The cold call is the most hated part of selling. It is the process of calling people and business to find out they may like your product or service. Cold calling is dreaded by both the sales person and he people who may be interrupted to answer.

Commercial Buyers

A commercial buyers works for a business or corporation. Commercial buyers deal with all aspects of buying for the business. A commercial buyer may negotiate a big discount in exchange for purchasing hundreds or even thousands of units.

Commercial Market

This is also known as a business, or industrial, market and is one where companies buy goods or services for consumption in their business or to transform the goods into other products to be sold

Commission

Commission is the revenue paid to the salesperson or company at the completion of a sale. Different industries have varying commission structures. A small commission may be 5%, while a good commission may be 15% or more.

Communication Channel

Elements within the Promotions Mix that an organization uses to communicate with target audiences (See Promotions Mix)

Communications Research

Research aspects of promotions decisions. Cooper identifies 4 key areas [1]: effectiveness research, media selection, copy testing and sales force effectiveness

Comparative Advertising

A technique that is illegal in some countries. A head to head advertising method that a business uses to compare their product to their competition and gauge the marketability of their product.

Competition-Based Pricing

CBP is a method of pricing a business product against its perceived value of other brands.

Competitive Advantage

Using all the products advantages and popularity to be in a better position than the competition. The term USP (Unique Selling Proposition) helps the increase it' public appeal.

Competitive Parity

Where businesses mirror other businesses or larger companies to hold a steady price as the market leader. The goal is to prevent a price war between the smaller companies forcing both to lose business.

Competitors

Competitors are anyone that sells the same product or provides the same services as you do. Within your market or geographical area. Your market research on your competition must be done on a regular basis.

Concentrated Strategy

A concentrated strategy is a marketing strategy that tailors marketing to a certain niche market or specific group. Mothers day or fathers day may be a specific group that is marketed to.

Concession Close

The concession close is the salesperson last ditch effort to encourage the buyer to sign now. It is a special concession that the salesperson has held back in the event he needed to sweeten the deal.

Confirmatory Questions

Questions repeated to confirm that the seller in on track and able to fill the buyers needs.

Consumer

An individual who uses a product or service (they may not be the buyer)

Consumer Buyer Behavior

The process and the factors that influence buying. Factors influencing consumer buyer Behavior include: Personal factors (such as situation, demographics etc.), social (such as reference groups, role) and psychological (such as learning, attitude, personality); also the marketing environment and firms" marketing mixes.

Corporate Hospitality

Corporate VIP treatment of people associated with the company like Shareholders. Added perks to holding a position within the company structure.

Corporate Identity

The company brand which includes names, symbols, logos, color's, typefaces; the identify aims to reinforce the Corporate Image.

Corporate Image

The personality of the company as perceived by the public. For instance you would get differing opinions when asked about Wal-Mart verses Disney. The public Identity of Wal-Mart is that it is an evil empire. Disney is a fun place to bring the family.

Corporate Strategy

This is the long-term plan for the company as laid out in their business plan.

Cross Selling

Selling different parts of a product range, that they have not previously brought, to an existing customer

Cultural Empathy

When a salesperson or a company achieves a rapport, or understanding, of a customer's culture

Culture

Our culture involves everything around us. it is very complex and includes our language, religion, education, social Behavior, politics and social attitudes.

Customer Loyalty

The loyalty established customers have to a company. They are always willing to back their business to shop time after time.

Customer Philosophy

Ranking the customer first, always trying to meet the customers needs.

Customer Relationship Management (CRM)

The planning, implementation and control of all interactions with customers, clients and sales prospects.

Customer Service

The time and attention put in by a company to make sure each customer is satisfied.

D

Data Processing

Digitally obtaining, recording and maintaining information, which can be retrieved and used

Database Marketing

Stored information about customers so that specific groups can be selected and targeted for marketing activity

Dealing With Objections

If there is an objection that comes up time and time again, the salesperson may raise it themselves and counter it. This means that they control its timing but, of course, it may be something the prospect hadn't thought about

Decider

The Decider makes the final decision regarding the product or service to be bought. They are often the experts and/or CFO, owner.

Demographic Segmentation

Breaking down the marketing into demographics. Age, race, religion, income.\

Demography

Information profiling a population in terms of their age, gender, income, stage in the family life cycle, religion and social class; is frequently used for segmenting consumer markets. A business's demography relates to its age, size and type of industry

Desk Research

Collecting data from existing sources and using that which already exists. Also known as Secondary Research.

Differential Advantage

Advantages a corporation may have other another. An example is a large corporation able to buy in bulk lots and sell for less that their competition.

Differentiated Strategy

Where a firm targets many segments with a different marketing mix for each segment

Direct Close

The most direct route to a close, Asking point blank for their business.

Direct Mail

Targeting a mass of people through mailers, postcards or flyers.

Direct Marketing

Direct Marketing is the process of marketing directly to potential customers without advertisements or through radio, TV or print. Physical materials are sent out directly to consumers to inform them of the product or service.

Direct Response Advertising (DRA)

Any type of advertising that solicits a response by potential customers. Such as an email reply, phone call, return coupon, one click on Internet. The consumer is urged to act now for a special deal.

Discrimination Pricing

This is where a business has different pricing for different people. Pricing varies according to their demographic.

Distribution

The physical distribution and management through various outlets and channels that have been set up to carry a product line.

Distribution Channel

Channeling goods from their distribution center to the various channels or outlets they have around the country.

Distribution Research

3 key areas warehouse research, transportation research, retail outlet research. Each section is research to find the best strategy for a certain product.

Distribution Strategy

There are 3 strategies: Intensive, Selective, and Exclusive. Each strategy is customized for each product to get the best market exposure possible.

Distributor

Distributors tend to buy in bulk, break bulk and sell and distribute to retailers, the trade or end users.

Diversification

A marketing strategy that a firm may pursue to develop new products in new markets

Domestic Buyers

Those who buy for their own consumption. This often involves more emotion than logic, although logic may still play a part. Factors influencing domestic buyers are: frequency, importance, social class.

Domestic Market

The domestic market is where consumers buy for personal use.

E

Early Payment Discount

A discount is offered if payment is made prior to pre arranged payment date.

E-commerce

Selling goods electronically, usually over the Internet

E-marketing

Using electronic means such as e-mail and the Internet; incorporates e-commerce and promotion to market your product or business.

Electronic Point of Sale (EPOS)

Electronic cash registers that store information into a database. This machine also compiles reports on inventory, menu popularity, traffic, billing and so on.

Empathy Statements

A simple way for a salesperson to show that he understands the problem of his customer and is ready and able to help.

Endorsement

An endorsement usually comes from a former athlete, celebrity, public figure or satisfied customer and is powerful in bolstering customer confidence.

Ethics

The moral ethics you work by in your business practice. A valued set of principles.

Ethical Selling and Marketing

Sales and Marketing are becoming increasingly important in sales and marketing. The basis for which people will base their trust in your word.

Exclusive Distribution

A limited distribution strategy for the purpose of being 'one of a kind' or 'exclusive.

External Analysis

Evaluation the external sales and marketing environment, such as political, legal, economic, social and technological factors. These factors are usually outside the control of the firm

Extranet

An intranet that is accessible to authorized external users.

Eye Gestures

A persons eyes movement up and down or side to side. Both have a significant meaning in body language.

F

Family Life Cycle

The stages an individual goes through during their life egg single, married no children, married with young children and so on.

Feature

A selling feature about a given product. Can be its size, durability, color, and portability.

Field Research

This is first time research also called primary research. The three types of primary research are: surveys, observation and experimentation

Field Selling (or Marketing)

When a company sends a representative into the field to meet on location with a business owner or company.

Financier

The businessperson in charge of finances.

FMCGs

Low price products, that have a fast turnover and, usually, short life, such as packaged food, toiletries and tobacco products.

Focus Groups

A select group of people brought in by a company to test, and use a product. The focus group then reports its findings back to the company.

Forecasting

Estimating or calculating future events and performances. This includes sales forecasting, market forecasting or technological forecasting.

Four P's

Four controllable variables, known as 'the 4 Ps': product, place price and promotion;

Franchise

A business owner (franchisee) buys a license to sell a product or service from its owner (the franchisor). The franchisee usually pays a fee and royalties and the franchisor allows use of a brand name, may provide marketing and support. Papa John's pizza is a franchise.

Franchisee

The person who buys the franchise i.e. the right to use the franchise name

Franchisor

The company, or person, who is the principal and sells the right to use the name etc. to the franchisee.

G

Geodemographics

Analyzing and segmenting markets by a combination of geographic and demographic variables.

Geographic Segmentation

A method of segmentation where the market is classified by where they live or are located.

Grey Market

Polite way of defining an elderly population although the grey market is becoming more healthy, wealthy and "youthful"

Group Communication

Selling to a group of people. Planning and preparation, setting meeting objectives that are acceptable to the group, consider variations in the group's mode of communication establish group body language, involve everyone.

Guarantees

A legal commitment by a company to repair, replace or compensate for faulty goods and services

H

Hard Fact Questions

Question that probe the inside facts or an organization such as company size, employees and the like.

Honesty Gestures

These indicate whether a person is telling the truth but need to be used with care. If the person is not being honest they will often put their hand to their face, scratch their nose or neck

House-to-House Distribution

A company that delivers directly to a consumer's house. An example is Amazon.

I

Ice-Break

This is where the salesperson should put both themselves and the prospect at ease and start to build a rapport. In a domestic sales situation this may take ten to fifteen minutes, a business sales situation should be shorter, normally no more than five minutes

Inbound Enquiry

A potential customer wanting to know more about your product or service.

Incentives

An enticement for a consumer to increase the attraction of buying a good or service. These can be in the form of a sales promotion such as free gifts, upgrade or any other special selling perk.

Industrial Marketing

Also known as Business-to-Business (B2B) marketing where a firm markets goods or services to another organization

Influencer

Influencers may be people from inside or outside the purchasing firm but have influence over decision makers regarding the product/company that is bought. They are often consultants.

Initiator

The business representative that starts the buying process.

Intermediary

A third party consultant or broker that works with the company and the buyers.

Internal Analysis

A report and analyses of the company's internal situation such as people, resources, products and marketing effort. This date is then used to make adjustments in the company's forward movement.

Internal Customers

Internal customers are employees. All employees should be viewed as customers.

Internal Marketing

The in house marketing plan that company employees are able to use when talking about their company.

International Sales and Marketing

Sales and marketing of goods and services to overseas countries

Intranet

An internal network used to share information. Used in-house by different departments in the company.

K

Key Account Management

A key Account is a high profile company that a company works with, a big buyer or product. Key accounts usually have a specific person in the company that talks to them directly like the business owner. They are VIP accounts.

Kinesthetic Communication

Kinesthetic involves touching and feeling; this in not the visual and audio person and they tend to be driven by emotion. These buyers tend to like multiple handshakes, arm touching, shoulder pats and the like.

L

Lead

A potential customer interested in your product or service.

Learning Log

Part of a Personal Development Plan keep by an employee.

Log Book

Diary of actions to be undertaken, usually for a week, broken into half-hour sections

Logo

A visual symbol that identifies a company or brand. It usually comprises a name, logo and symbols and should be consistent in its use.

Loss leader

Is a phrase used in retailing. It is a product that is sold at a low price (either at break-even or at a loss) in order to attract customers into the store.

M

Macro Environment

The wider environment, or external factors, that impact a firm's business, sales and marketing; they are usually beyond the firm's control.

Mailing Preference Service (MPS)

A database of addresses of consumers that have requested not to be sent unsolicited direct mail. It is illegal not to abide by this.

Margin

The profit made from a product or service. A percentage made after the break-even point.

Market-Based Pricing

This includes strategies where the major consideration is pricing a product based on what the market considers it to be worth and is prepared to pay.

Market Development

A marketing strategy of taking an existing product to new markets.

Market Entry

Where a firm launches a new product into a new or existing market.

Market Penetration

When a business decides to sell more on one product in existing markets. Expanding the market or increasing product usage.

Market Research

Gathering, analyzing data about the market to reduce risk and enable better marketing decisions to be made. It includes: estimates of market size and potential, identification of key market characteristics and segments, forecasting market trends and gathering information on existing and potential customers.

Market Segmentation

The identification and classification of meaningful buyer groups in order to target selected segments and develop a relevant marketing mix. Market segmentation is the first stage of the Target Marketing Process. Consumer markets may be segmented by: geographics, demographics, geodemographics, psychographics, buyer Behavior.

Market Share

How a company gauges the saturation of their product in a given market. Their share is the percentage as compared to their competition.

Marketing

Marketing is the management process responsible for identifying, anticipating and satisfying customer requirements profitably.

Marketing Communications

Techniques that an organization may use to communicate with specified target audiences. It includes advertising, PR, sales promotion and personal selling and is also known as the "Promotion" element of the marketing mix

Marketing Information

Information that is obtained and stored to enable a firm to make effective marketing decisions: it differs from data as it is processed data and, therefore, more meaningful.

Marketing Mix

Marketing variables that a firm uses in order to deal with the marketing environment. It is called a "mix" as all elements must work effectively together to reflect a product of firm's positioning. The mix for products involves four controllable variables, known as 'the 4 Ps': product, place, price and promotion; the mix for services, known as the 7 Ps", is people, process and 'physical evidence, product, place, price and promotion

Marketing Planning

A plan to identify and pursue specific market segments by offering relevant products and services. The plan includes an analysis, objectives, strategies, tactics, implementation, and controls

Marketing Research

Gathering and analyzing data about any internal and external factors to reduce risk and enable better marketing decisions to be made. It includes: market research, product research, pricing research, distribution research, promotions research, sales research, and environmental research. It should not be confused with Market Research, which involves research the market only and is just one aspect of marketing research

Market Skimming

Charging a high price for an exclusive product

Marketing Strategy

The strategic, or long-term, marketing plan

Markup

The profit from a product or service stated as a percentage of the cost of producing the product or service. It is often confused with Margin, which is the profit from a product or service stated as a percentage of the selling price

Mass Market

A very large segment or wide collection of smaller segments

Media Release

Press materials release to the media Radio, TV, print for the purpose of a promotion or sale.

Micro Environment

The external environment that impacts a firm's business, sales and marketing. It is closer to the firm than the macro-environment.

Mirroring

It involves adopting similar body language, stances and gestures to the other person: mirroring leads to a state of rapport

Mission Statement

A firm's business philosophy and direction; it is used to help a firm to develop its long-term plan

Mystery Shopper

Someone hired to shop at a business posed as a customer. They report back to the company on their experience.

N

NASA

An acronym meaning Need, Acceptance, Solution, Acceptance.

Need Identification

The single most important aspect of any selling situation and it is universally recognized that if the salesperson does not know the real need, or problem, they cannot offer the true benefits to help resolve the situation.

New Business Development

The acquisition of new customers

New Product Development (NPD)

The development of new products and involves research, development, product testing, test marketing and launch

Niche Market

A small or narrow market segment

Non-Verbal Communication

Non-verbal communication. Body language, which includes the way you stand or sit, facial expressions, gesticulations, how you hold your head and use your eyes

O

Objection

A challenge to or rejection by a prospect feature or benefit of a firm, product or service. It may occur at any time during the sales process and the salesperson should be prepared to counter these.

Objection Close

The salesperson states that if the objection can be overcome will the buyer place the order. Used when a potential buyer has made an objection.

Objectives

Specific, measurable, achievable, relevant and times aims. A firm will usually have overall business objectives (relating to profit), marketing objectives (relating to market share, revenue, products and markets) and sales objectives relating (to revenue broken down by product, geographic area and individual sales people).

OEM (Original Equipment Manufacturer)

A Company that supplied equipment to other companies to resell or incorporate into another product using the reseller's brand name.

One Level Distribution Channel

The Producer sells to the consumer (business or domestic) via one intermediary, egg a distributor or retailer

Open Gestures

These are a positive form of body language where a person does not appear to be protecting their body and so they do not have their legs crossed or arms folded. To be read as open to ideas and a sales pitch.

Open Ended Questions

Questions in marketing research that allows the person to answer as they see fit. They provide qualitative data. They start with words such as Who? What? Where? How? Why? When?

Operational Efficiency

Not wasting money so savings can be spent directly on the customer (through low prices), or indirectly (through product quality or investment in technology)

Orientation

A firm's culture

Outbound Call Center

Their main function is to make telemarketing calls; they are also called Sales Call centers

P

Packaging

Part of both the Product element of the Marketing Mix and Promotions element. Provides functional benefits of protection and communications function of brand identity, awareness at the point of sale and a reminder in the home; also, often has a legal function

Paraphrasing

Repeating what is said in your own words to ensure the message is understood

PDP-Personal Development Plan.

A plan developed by an individual that assesses their strengths, weaknesses, opportunities and threats. S.W.O.T.

Penetration Pricing

Strategy whereby a firm charges a low price in order to increase sales.

Personal Space

The area around an individual that they do not wish to be invaded: it tends to vary between personal and business situations

P.E.S.T

Political, Economic, Socio-cultural and Technological - a way of defining the macro environment.

Physical Evidence

One of the 7Ps of the extended Marketing Mix for services.

Place

The Distribution element of the marketing mix. It involves the process of getting the goods from the supplier to the user and involves channel management and physical distribution management.

Positive Mental Attitude

A frame of mind, which considers solutions rather than problems

Point of Sale (POS)

This is also known as POP, Point of Purchase. It usually relates to retail outlets and includes where goods are located, displays, stands and signs to draw attention.

Portfolio

The range of products or services that a company offers to its customers

Positioning

The third stage of the target marketing process following segmentation and targeting. It is the creation of an image for a firm, product, service or brand as compared with competitors.

Post-Sale

After the sale, the follow up. It also comprises those activities that are undertaken by a salesperson after an actual sales takes place. Includes processing the order and follow-up. Post-sale follows pre-sale and the sale stages.

Premium Pricing

Another name for Prestige Pricing. A pricing strategy whereby a firm charges a high price because of the (perceived) quality and image of the product.

Preparation

Gather information and facts prior to a meeting or conference. Knowing all you can about the company, the person, the product and the industry.

Pre-Sale

The Pre-Sale includes prospecting, appointment making and preparation, including research. Pre-sale precedes the sale and post-sale stages

Presentation

The presentation is where the salesperson sells the benefits of the product or service supported by its features. They should convince the prospect that their product will in some way make their life better.

Prestige Pricing

A pricing strategy whereby a firm charges a high price because of the (perceived) quality and image of the product and/or brand. Also known as Premium Pricing

Pricing Research

Research in order to determine the optimum price

Primary Research

Also known as Field Research. This is research that is being undertaken for the first time, as opposed to Secondary Research. The three types of primary research are: surveys, observation and experimentation.

Problem Identification

The single most important aspect of any selling situation and it is the salesperson finding out the real need, or problem, so they can offer the true benefits to help resolve the situation. Problem Identification is tied into NASA: Need, Acceptance, Solution, Acceptance

Processes Segmentation

A method of business segmentation where the market is classified according to processes it uses, such as the level of technology

Product Life Cycle

The stages a product goes through from pre-launch to withdrawal from the market: most commonly, there are four and five stage models. The four stage model: introduction, growth, maturity and decline The five stage model: development, introduction, growth, maturity, decline

Product Orientation

A product oriented company to be one where the firm puts product excellence and/or technology first. Some firms, such as pharmaceutical companies may have little choice as what they develop depends on technological breakthroughs

Production Orientation

A philosophy of business whereby the firm's focus is on product excellence or technology. May be necessary in a highly technological environment.

Product Research

Generation of new product ideas, testing ideas, developing prototypes, testing prototypes, test marketing, Adjusting the marketing mix prior to launch

Professional Services

The services provided by firms and individuals that are qualified and/or accredited by professional bodies, such as accountants, solicitors, surveyors and chartered marketers.

Promotions Mix

All marketing communications tools that are used together, to achieve communications objectives in relation to specific target audiences. The mix varies according to objectives, target audiences and budget and may include: advertising, personal selling, sales literature, public relations, direct marketing, sales promotion, packaging, point of sale and product placement.

Public Relations

The planning and implementation of communication activities to establish and maintain the reputation of a firm and its brands, within identified target audiences, often including the general public.

Q

Qualify

Where a sales person establishes purchasing potential of a prospect and also determines that the person they are talking to has the relevant decision-making authority

Quantity Discount

Is a reduction in price to the buyer for buying a specific quantity: often, the larger the quantity, the more the discount

Questioning Techniques

The use of effective questioning skills to establish a prospects needs. Cooper [1] indicates that these should include: listen more than talk, ask open questions, use confirmatory closed questions, ask soft and hard fact questions and use empathy statements (see relevant sections)

Question the Objection (Method of Dealing With Objections)

If a prospect raises a vague objection it can be difficult to deal with: the salesperson needs to find out the specific issue, which may actually be very small egg if they say a product is awful ask what specific aspect they dislike.

R

Rapport

Developing empathy with the customer: Cooper [1] identities three inputs to rapport: create an environment of ease, establish common ground, and use similar communication signals

Recommended Retail Price (RRP)

The price at which a company recommends their retailers sells the item to the consumer. Since the 1960s it has been illegal, in most cases, to force retailers to sell at this price

R&D

Research and development: a function undertaken to develop new products

Reference Group

Those groups with which a customer identifies in some way and they can have a positive or negative influence on their buyer Behavior. Examples include those whose opinions are valued such as sports personalities, also families, friends and work colleagues

Referral

A prospect, or lead, provided to a salesperson as being someone who may be interested in what the salesperson is selling

Retailer

An outlet, and part the distribution chain, that sells directly to consumers Return on Investment (ROI)

Retrospective Discount

Is payment made back to the buyer at the end of an agreed period if the total purchases for that period reach an agreed amount. Is used when the buyer does not know, in advance, the quantity required for the period

Reverse Psychology

In sales this tends to be used on a reluctant or hesitant buyer, where the salesperson gives them the benefits of not buying. It is a technique that must be used with care

S

Sale

A major stage in the sales cycle and comprises those activities that are undertaken by a salesperson during an actual sales visit or on the telephone: typically includes ice break and rapport, needs/problem identification, presentation, negotiation, handling objections, closing. It follows pre-sale activity and preceded post-sale activity

Sales Call center

These are premises where many telephone lines are routed into numerous telephone operators who work at the call center, usually using headsets and computers. They may operate on behalf of one organization, or be contracted to many. Being sales call centers, they not only receive calls but their main function is to make telemarketing calls; they are also called Outbound Call centers

Sales Cycle

A complete process, which can be applied in the selling environment. Different texts indicate a different number of stages although they all tend to follow the same pattern, even though some stages may occur at any time during the sales process.

Sales Orientation

A philosophy of business whereby the firm's focus is on selling, rather than the customer.

Sales Promotion

One element of the Promotions Mix and involves a range of temporary inducements that includes: coupons, free gifts, competitions, BOGOF (buy one get one free), temporary interest free credit and so on. Trade sales promotions are an important form of push strategy and may include temporary interest free credit, sale or return, free promotional material, extra boxes free

Sales Revenue

The income made by a firm before any deductions have been made. Sales revenue from an individual order is calculated as Price times Volume

Secondary Research

Also known as Desk Research. This involves collecting data from existing sources and so using that which already exists, as opposed to Primary Research. Secondary sources include internal sources and external sources, such as the internet, government statistics, trade directories and so on. There are several potential problems associated with secondary research but it is often plentiful and free, or inexpensive

Selective Distribution

A distribution strategy involving a firm limiting the number of outlets it sells its products from possibly because of special storage or knowledge requirements, legal requirements or just because consumers would be willing to travel to buy the goods

Self-Evaluation

When the salesperson evaluates their own performance regarding what they did well and what they could have done better

Selling

Personal communication between a seller and (prospective) purchaser. As well as a critical role in itself, it can be considered part of the Promotions function of the

Marketing Mix. Cooper defines selling as "a function which is concerned with identifying the specific needs, desires and problems of individual customers and providing satisfaction of these through benefit or solution in order to facilitate profitable business transactions"

Self-Motivation

The ability to enable a sales person to have the desire to do well; it is enhanced by having a positive mental attitude. Cooper [1] identifies four key factors to help develop self-motivation: belief in oneself, belief in the product or service, self-evaluation, having a driving force

Segmentation

Also known as Market Segmentation. The identification and classification of meaningful buyer groups. Segmentation is the first stage of the Target Marketing process. Consumer markets may be segmented by: geographics, demographics, geodemographics, psychographics, buyer Behavior Business markets may be segmented by: geographics, demographics, processes, their markets, buyer Behavior (See relevant sections)

Segmentation Pricing

A pricing strategy whereby a firm charges different prices for different market segments. Is also called Discrimination Pricing

Service Level Agreement

A legal part of a contract that states a guaranteed level of service; it often includes penalties for not achieving those levels of service

Service (Marketing)

A service is an intangible product that has five key characteristics that create problems for the marketer and sales person; these are: intangibility (it cannot be seen or touched); Inseparability (it is produced and consumed at the same time); Heterogeneity (it is inconsistent in quality as it relies on people delivering the service); Perishability (it cannot be stored); Lack of Ownership (it cannot be owned). These problems lead the marketer to extend the Marketing Mix for services to the 7Ps, rather than the 4Ps as for products

Seven Ps

The Marketing Mix for services. The "mix" is all elements that must work effectively together to reflect a product of firm's positioning.

Skimming/ Skim-The Cream Pricing

A pricing strategy where the firm sets the price high in the early stages of the product life cycle to cover high development costs and achieve as much profit as possible before prices are driven down by competitors entering the market or new technologies overtaking. Is a common strategy in electronics markets where "innovators" are prepared to pay a high price for a new technology.

Smoke Screen

An artificial objection that a prospect states to either divert the salesperson from addressing the primary objection.

Social Class

Also known as Socio-Economic Group. A classification of people who have similar levels of wealth defined through the types of job they do.

Societal Marketing Concept

A business philosophy which takes into account the interests of society as a whole as well as aiming to satisfy the needs of the customer

Socio-Economic Group

Also known as Social Class. A classification of people who have similar levels of wealth defined through the types of job they do. There are various ways of defining social class: marketers sometimes used this as a method of demographic segmentation and normally use those identified by the media where the classes are defined as A, B, C1, C2, D and E. An example is those in social class A are defined as "Upper middle class" and comprise senior managers such as MDs, barristers, surgeons and so on. This method of segmentation is increasingly having less credibility than others.

Soft Fact Questions

These questions probe regarding opinion, feelings and thoughts

Spin

Where a firm aims to use or manipulate the media to their advantage; often through PR. Tends to have negative connotations

Sponsorship

A form of Promotion, often considered PR, where a firm provides support for an event, venture, person or charity in order to obtain positive publicity.

Stakeholders

Those people and organizations that have some interest in a business and/or the business has an interest in them. Stakeholders may include: shareholders, employees, members of the local community, customers, suppliers, intermediaries, local or national government, local publics, regulatory bodies

Standard Industrial Classifications (SIC)

Codes used to group businesses according to the type of industry they are in.

STEEPLE

An alternative mnemonic to PEST, PESTLE or SLEPT for macro environmental analysis; it stands for Socio- cultural, Technological, Economic, Environmental, Political, Legal and E-business.

Straight Denial (Method of Dealing With Objections)

This involves informing the prospect that they are mistaken. It can be used when the objection is inaccurate but should be used carefully, as the sales person may appear aggressive.

Strategic Orientation

Where a firm thinks and plans for the long-term and has a marketing person at senior management level to be the champion of the customer; this also enables resources to be allocated for the benefit of the customer

Summarization

A part of need identification in the sales process when a salesperson must check back with the prospect to confirm that all needs and desires have been covered and understood [1]

Supply Chain

The chain or network from suppliers, manufacturers, distributors and other intermediaries involved in the production and delivery of a product to the final consumer

Suspect

An individual or firm that has the potential to be a prospect but with whom the salesperson has not yet made contact

Survey

A method of collecting data where the researcher makes a systematic record of responses from all respondents who have answered the same questions

SWOT Analysis

A technique of analysis, which studies Strengths, Weaknesses, Opportunities and Threats. This can be undertaken for a firm, as part of their sales and marketing plans, or an individual as part of their PDP (Personal Development Plan) and can be developed from a detailed audit

T

Target Marketing

The process of Segmentation, Targeting and Positioning; not to be confused with Market Targeting, which is the full name for Targeting, the second stage in the Target Marketing Process. Segmentation, the first stage, involves the identification and classification of meaningful buyer groups. Segmentation is the first stage of the Target Marketing process. Consumer markets may be segmented by: geo-graphics, demographics, geo-demographics, psychographics, buyer Behavior

Telemarketing

The marketing of a product or service directly to a customer by telephone: this may be involving sales, research or customers care

Tele-selling

Selling goods or services directly to a customer through use of the telephone

Test Marketing

The testing of the Marketing Mix of a product in a sample area prior to a full launch

Third Party Endorsement

Where a person, who has nothing to gain by the transaction, recommends the firm, product or brand to potential customers. The most valuable are experts or those who have experience of the product or service

Total Quality Management (TQM)

Focuses on satisfaction of customer needs in combination with the achievement of objectives and covers: quality, availability, service, support, reliability, value for money and needs to consider: the customer, corporate planning, management, personnel, physical evidence.

Thoughtful Gestures

These show that the person is considering something and tend to be hand to head gestures, such as rubbing the head or scratching the chin; the sales person should not interrupt these

Trade Marketing

Marketing of goods and services to the retail and distributive trades

Trade Buyers

Those who buy on behalf of an intermediary in order to sell on. This involves more logic than emotion, although emotion still plays a part. Factors influencing trade buyers are: price, bulk purchase, quality, repeat business, payment terms, availability of just in time .See also Business Buyer Behavior

Trial Close (Method of Dealing With Objections)

If the salesperson feels that the timing is right and the buyer has just one objection left, they can try to turn it into a trial close. A trial close is where the salesperson tries to close the sale but, if it doesn't work, it doesn't prevent him from continuing with the selling process. The salesperson would possibly ask that if they could overcome the objection would the prospect place the order

Two Level Distribution Channel

The Producer sells to the consumer (business or domestic) via two intermediary, eggs a distributor and then on to a retailer

Undifferentiated Strategy

One of three target marketing strategies. It is where the firm targets many segments but with one overall marketing mix

Unique Selling Point (USP)

Also known a Unique Selling Preposition (USP). A feature or features that no other competitive product/service has [1]. Sales and marketing people should be aware of the USP of all their products, as it is critical in a product's success

Unique Selling Preposition (USP)

Also known as Unique Selling Point. A feature or features that no other competitive product/service has [1]. Sales and marketing people should be aware of the USP of all their products, as it is critical in a product's success.

Value Added Reseller (VAR)

Similar to an OEM but is usually used in reference to software companies. Unlike some OEMs, VARs always add something extra to the product or service

Viral Marketing

Spreading a brand message using word of mouth, or via e-mail, originating from the firm although this is not apparent. Examples of techniques include: jokes, film clips, games and website addresses: they are suitably interesting to be forwarded to others

Vision

The long-term aspirations of a firm

W

Weekly Log

Diary of actions to be undertaken for the forthcoming week, broken into half-hour sections.

What The Market Will Bear

A pricing strategy whereby a firm charges what the market is able and/or prepared to pay: it may be a high or low price and is frequently used in business-to-business marketing.

Wholesaler

Also known as a distributor. Tend to buy in bulk, break bulk and sell and distribute to retailers, the trade or end users. Except for cash and carry wholesalers they give credit and transport to their customers. Many large retailers have undertaken Vertical Integration and developed their own wholesaling system

WIIFM

Recognized sales acronym meaning what's in it for me? If a sales person is asked this it means that they have only sold in features and not benefits

Z

Zero-Level Distribution Channel

The Producer sells direct to the consumer (business or domestic) and so there are no intermediaries